MW00396149

Walking Through Cancer

By
GERMAINE J. HOFFMAN

But Jesus looked at them and said,
"With men it is impossible,
but not with God; for with God
all things are possible."
Mark 10:27

COPYRIGHT © 2017 GERMAINE J. HOFFMAN
WALKING THROUGH CANCER
By Germaine J. Hoffman

All Scripture quotations, unless otherwise noted, are taken from the New King James Version®. Copyright © 1982 by Thomas Nelson, Inc. Used by permission. All rights reserved.

Scripture quotations marked NLT are taken from the Holy Bible, New Living Translation. Copyright © 1996, 2004, 2007. Used by permission of Tyndale House Publishers, Inc., Carol Stream, Illinois 60188. All rights reserved.

Scripture quotations marked NIV are taken from The Holy Bible, New International Version® NIV®, Copyright © 1973, 1978, 1984, 2011 by Biblica Inc. Used by permission of Zondervan Bible Publishers. All rights reserved worldwide.

Scripture quotations identified KJV are from the King James Version of the Bible.

All rights reserved. No part of this book may be used or reproduced by any means, graphic, electronic, or mechanical, including photocopying, recording, taping or by any information storage retrieval system without the written permission of the publisher except in the case of brief quotations embodied in critical articles and reviews.

Jesus said to Germaine,
"Daughter, your faith has made you well.
Go in peace. Your suffering is over."

Mark 5:34 NLT

Special Thanks to:
Mary Walsh, cover photography
Jeff Hoffman, cover design
Darla Bonk and Lisa Sadler, editors
Joy Rocco, formatter

CONTENTS

Dedicated With Love and Appreciation...

To my amazing husband, Jeff, whom I love with all of my heart: you have been my "Rock," my strength, and my help at all times. Our marriage of 34 years and love for one another continues to grow stronger every day. I thank and praise God for giving me such a loving, kind, godly, inspiring, faith-filled man such as you. You truly have been the wind beneath my wings helping me to overcome every hurdle, encouraging me to go on at my physical weakest, and being a true source of strength on every level. You were faithful in prayer and had great faith to believe that God would completely heal me of stage 4 lung cancer for nonsmoking women when all of the medical odds were against us. Thank you for your obedience to God when He spoke and directed you to, "Stretch out your hand and I will heal her." I am blessed beyond measure to be your wife. Forever I love you. Forever I am yours. I am so thankful that you are mine!

To our Lord and Savior Jesus Christ, the Head of our life and marriage: Jeff and I are so grateful for our covenant relationship with You. You are the strongest part of our relationship, and we rely completely upon You. You have carried us through the hard times and continue to bless us with Your peace and presence. We could have never made it through the trials of life or stage 4 lung cancer without Your love and grace. Our heartfelt "thank you" seems inadequate for all You have done; but we are forever grateful for Your mercy that has kept us united, restored my body, and brought us over the victory line! May You be glorified in every word and page of this book. To You be the glory for the great things You have done! May others come to trust and believe in You as their Lord and Savior.

To my amazing team of doctors: Dr. Harwin (Oncologist), Dr. Challapalli (Pulmonologist), Dr. Sandadi (Gynecologic Oncologist), Dr. Syed (Primary Care Physician), Maurine & Dawn (Physical Therapists), and all of the wonderful nurses and staff (too many to name) that helped us through this journey—thank you!

To my wonderful siblings: sisters Debbie, Kathy, and Eileen; my big brothers Bob and David; my sister-in-loves Vicky, Barb, and Ann; my brother-in-loves Doug, Lenny, and Kurt—thank you!

To my countless devoted friends, church family, Facebook friends, and ALL who prayed for me all over this globe, thank you!

The effective, fervent prayer of a righteous man avails much.
James 5:16b
🕊️

Special tribute to Rhonda Christine Hardy my dear sister in the Lord and beloved friend. She fought the good fight, finished her race, and kept the faith.
She has her heavenly reward. I will always love and miss her.
Well done, good and faithful servant…

Foreword

Getting the devastating news that my wife had stage 4 lung cancer for nonsmoking women was unreal. Up to that point, I was used to a perfectly healthy wife who enjoyed taking walks, riding bikes, or going to the beach. Her health record was impeccable. There were only a handful of times she would catch the common cold or experience a slight headache. Suddenly, the scales massively tipped on the opposite side of the health chart, and her minor incidents of sickness escalated to the major "C" word that no one ever wants to hear.

Unexpectedly, the night of her diagnosis, God woke me up at 3:00 a.m. and I heard Him clearly tell me, "Stretch out your hand and I will heal her." It was like a Father talking to his son in a very intimate way. God's powerful words of instruction and His loving promise to heal my bride gave me the peace and assurance I needed to know my girl would be all right.

His words also stirred a rush of personal emotions from deep within me which brought joy to my heart and tears to my eyes. God knows how much I love my wife and He wanted me to know that He loves her, too. In that moment, I experienced God's love firsthand in a truly meaningful and humbling way. I searched the Bible for an appropriate healing Scripture and the Lord led me to this verse...

> *But Jesus turned Him about, and when He saw her, He said,*
> *"Daughter, be of good comfort; thy faith hath made thee whole."*
> *And the woman was made whole from that hour.*
> Matthew 9:22 KJV
> 🕊

God's personal Word to me and His promise to heal my wife were major players in my own healing. Faith, hope, love, prayer and Scripture took me through the challenging time of caring for my bride minute by minute, hour by hour, day by day, week by week, and month by month.

Though she endured many blood tests, CT scans, chemo treatments, and side effects, she still kept praising God the whole time. She thanked every nurse, doctor, lab worker, and medical staff member for taking care of her and helping her. Even during the toughest times, she chose to praise God more while always making the time to share her faith in God, and pray for and encourage others.

While I knew early on that God had the power to heal the love of my life, after reading all of the medical research, I also accepted the horrific fact that He might choose to take her home to Heaven (that's what happens when statistics show this type of cancer affects 232,000 people annually and offers a less than 1% survival rate). Listening to the almost hopeless medical outcome rather than listening to God can discourage the strongest believer.

I am a decision-maker and always consider all aspects of any given situation. When I contemplated the possibility of losing my wife, knowing she would be in Heaven made me feel slightly better (because I know there is no more suffering there). However, the thought of being alone here on earth, without my bride, and waiting my turn to be reunited with her again someday was frightening. Thankfully, when I began seeing major physical improvements on a daily basis, those fears began to subside. God lifted me and suddenly He was answering all of our prayers.

I need to interject an important point, though. Before the cancer diagnosis, I remember being discontent with my life at times. I prayed for God to do something "BIG"—never imagining this trial could be part of answering my prayers. I am not saying God allowed my wife to have cancer because I wanted a big change; but through the trial, He taught me how to be content and thankful for all of my blessings— BIG and small. God allowed cancer and suffering to enter our lives and used it to shift my focus to a much-needed Heavenly perspective. Everyday living became a gift I now chose to treasure and value in every moment of my life.

This is not just a story about a woman walking through cancer. It's about a happily married, God-loving couple walking through cancer.

Although my wife kept an amazing, uplifting attitude, more than once, she actually apologized for having cancer because it drastically changed our lives and way of living. Whenever she commented, "Honey, I am so sorry this happened." I instantly looked into her big beautiful brown eyes reminding her, "For better or worse...in sickness and in health..." When I made those vows at the altar 34 years ago, I meant them.

Through this process, we both learned many valuable lessons about life, love, and perseverance. Our struggles, as believers, can sometimes be harder than what others may experience, but we know, understand, and accept that suffering is part of being a Christian. We lay our lives down daily, remembering the great suffering Jesus endured to save us all as He shed His blood on the Cross as a sacrifice for our sins. Walking through cancer and shining Christ's light through the pain made His grace more evident to those around us who wanted to see how true believers live and respond to trials.

God's plan is perfect. He never promised us a trouble-free life, but He did promise to be with us in the trouble. His Word declares in John 16:33 NLT, "I have told you all this so that you may have peace in Me. Here on earth you will have **many trials** and sorrows. But take heart, because I have overcome the world." The trial builds us up on the inside and makes us stronger on the outside. It increases our faith and trust in God if we allow it to. Believers need to shine and show our best to those around us needing encouragement while equally sharing the struggles we experience. Others need to see the difference Jesus makes in our lives because the reward is so great—salvation, an abundant life here on earth, and eternity with God and our loved ones in Heaven! When we are weak, He is strong.

By the grace of God and the strength He gave us, separately and together, Germaine and I have inspired many. We tried to live so others would not only see how to talk the talk, but how to walk the walk of faith, love, and humility. For example, several young men from church who received the updates I wrote concerning my wife, individually emailed me saying when they meet the right woman, they aspire to be the kind of husband I am to my wife. This is a huge compliment and blessing, but I do not take it for granted. I know all of my help and strength comes from the Lord. They, too, will need to rely completely on Him.

I pray that this book will enlighten you, show you the miracle-working power of God, increase your faith, hope, and love, and most of all, make you want to be closer to Jesus than ever before.—*Jeff Hoffman*

Preface

Anyone who has ever walked through cancer knows that the struggle can be made easier with the help of a wonderful caregiver. My caregiver was my husband, Jeff. We have been married 34 years and he knows pretty much what I need and when I need it. But when I was diagnosed with stage 4 lung cancer for nonsmoking women, the Lord supernaturally anointed Jeff to know **exactly** what I needed when I needed it.

Let me give you a few examples: If I needed a tissue, my husband would already be handing it to me. If my neck hurt, even before I asked, he instinctively knew and came behind me to rub my neck and shoulders. If I needed encouragement, he was **ALWAYS** there cheering me on! He was so sensitive and tuned in to my every movement, emotion, and physical need while also being incredibly attentive to my spiritual needs.

Many times when I was sleeping, Jeff would lay his hands on me and pray for my healing and complete recovery. He also researched all of the medical information for endless hours and was able to intelligently engage in conversations with my doctors, especially my oncologist.

Jeff was extremely patient with me for months as my energy level dropped and it took an exorbitant amount of time for me to do "normal" things like getting out of bed in the morning, showering, picking out clothes to wear, getting dressed, brushing my teeth, putting on makeup, and doing my hair. Everything became a chore—I had slowed down to a snail's pace, but he patiently and lovingly waited until I was ready to get up and do things. Sometimes, to get things started, he brought me breakfast in bed—usually a protein shake or a bowl of cereal. I recall many times waking up at 8:00 a.m. and finally getting downstairs at almost noon. This is where the daily process continued—including deciding what to eat for lunch, taking my vitals (blood pressure, temperature, oxygen, and pulse levels), medications, and discussing what we would do for the day. Jeff never complained about any of it. That was true love in action—especially for my man. Those who know and love him, call him, "The man with the plan," because he likes to get things done with excellence and in a timely manner. The excellence was still there, but the timely manner went on vacation. My physical condition caused him to scale himself way back to adapt himself to his wife's 24/7 needs.

Yes, it definitely was a more than full-time job taking care of me. I thank God and Jeff from the bottom of my heart for doing it with so much excellence, love, and kindness.

Introduction

From the time I was a small child, I **knew** the call of God was on my life. I couldn't explain it, but there was always a "knowing" inside of me that I was made for great things—far beyond my natural abilities. I say that humbly, that the God who created Heaven and Earth was interested in me and had prearranged a great plan for my life. My mother used to tell me, "There is just something special about you!" She never pinpointed "the call" as the something special—but I knew in my heart that's what it was.

My parents took my siblings and me to church faithfully every week. There we were—the eight of us—my father, with my mother by his side, and the six children: Bobby, Debbie, Kathy, David, Eileen, and me, trailing behind my parents in single file as they escorted us to the front row of our large church. Even though our family faithfully attended church each week, I did not know the saving power of Jesus Christ until I was 23 years old.

Up to that point, my definition of a Christian meant being a good person, attending church, and knowing Jesus died for me. I was shocked to find out, **years later**, that my will was involved and I had a choice to make. Going to church is necessary, but that action alone did not automatically enroll me in the Lamb's Book of Life in Heaven, nor was it a qualifier for salvation. I came to realize that I had "head" knowledge of God, but I lacked the "heart" knowledge (living to please God). I reverenced His house, loved the Cross that was erected above the beautiful altar area, and heard messages about Him from the pulpit. But I did not know Him personally, although I always had the desire.

It wasn't until my friend and co-worker, Robin, shared the full Gospel of Christ with me that I learned how Jesus died for my salvation and the sins of the world. Mankind sinned against Holy God, and Jesus' sinless blood was the only sacrifice God would accept to restore us back to Himself. Jesus took our place and paid the ultimate price for abundant life on earth and eternity with Him in Heaven. She explained my need to repent of my sins, receive Jesus as my Lord and Savior, and then I would become part of the family of God. Once I received this information from Robin, I let it simmer on the back burner of my mind for a few weeks, but thank God the seed was planted on fertile and holy ground. My initial thought was, *"That's good for you, not for me."*

But life was about to change!

Thankfully, God knows everything. He sent Robin to deliver His message of love and faith to me before a medical shockwave rocked our world. You see, Jeff and I were just told that we could not physically have children. I was devastated, depressed, and feeling totally helpless and defeated! I thank God that Robin told me the message of salvation before we received our doctor's blow, "Mr. and Mrs. Hoffman, I am sorry to tell you, medically-speaking, it is impossible."

How could this happen to us? We were so young. I was 23 and Jeff was 26—it was only a few years after we married. Being a mom was all I ever wanted, and all I ever dreamed of (besides marrying my wonderful husband). This news felt like part of a bad dream that I did not want to come true.

Yet, I now know, sometimes the lowest times of our lives lead us to the highest places. My rock bottom made me more receptive to the Good News. God does use the foolish things to confound the wise. I was so down in the dumpster—only Jesus could lift me out! Now at my lowest point, it was good for me.

Only a few hours after receiving the doctor's devastating call about not being able to have children, with a broken heart, I fell to my knees in front of my bedroom dresser (which now became an altar). From the depth of my soul, I began crying the most grievous tears I have ever shed. I experienced a wide range of emotions from shock, disbelief, and sorrow, to great distress and quiet desperation. I cried out to Jesus as never before and pleaded to Him with everything within me, "Please come into my heart! Please forgive me for my sins! Please be my Lord and Savior!" And He did.

This prayer was the foundation to all other prayers I would ever pray. If God could save me by His grace and faith in Jesus' Name—I wondered, *"What else could He do?"*

Although I was now saved and on my way to Heaven, I spent many years quietly suffering through infertility, crying myself to sleep, and tearstaining countless pillow cases—while all of my girlfriends and family members went on to have children.

As I mourned my own loss, Mother's Day, baby showers, noticeably pregnant bellies, and birth announcements became unbearable. Countless well-meaning people continued asking the same rote questions, "When are you going to have children?" or "Do you have any children?" And, oh, the dreaded silence and strange look that repeatedly followed after hearing my response, "No, I don't."

How awkward! How painful! How lonely! It is a subject rarely touched on—even in the church. I was given the "Sarah and Abraham" scenario more times than I care to remember (Genesis 18:11—"Now Abraham and Sarah were old, well advanced in age; and Sarah had passed the age of childbearing.") Although Sarah eventually conceived the child of promise, trust me, that is the last thing a young, newly married, childless woman wants to hear after her dreams have been shattered.

Year after year, I believed things would change and God would come through. My church family always encouraged me to "take the rose," stand, or go to the altar on Mother's Day because I was a "spiritual" mom. Yes, I agree, it is an honor to be a spiritual mom, but they were missing the whole point. I wanted a child of my own and there was no substitute.

The next question was, "Did you ever think of adoption?" Oh my goodness, of course we did! We tried multiple times. We went to a well-known adoption agency and a faith-based agency. I was on a list at my gynecologist's office, but when we moved to a new home, they were unable to locate my new phone number and my doctor adopted out to another couple. A friend highly recommended us to a young pregnant woman who was interested in a private adoption. Only a few weeks into the process, however, she changed her mind and chose to give the baby to her best friend instead. (This scenario of starting the process, yet never coming to fruition, actually played out several different times.) A godly woman in our church, who ran a Christian adoption agency, contacted us, but we found out that we were unable to afford the dollar amount involved. All of these instances happened over the process of time, and there was always a NO each time we stepped out on faith, but it's never the wrong time to believe God for the right thing.

Childlessness is a devastating loss for those who want children. It is a grief and pain so deep that only the one experiencing it can describe the void, but even they can never fully understand it because it seems so unnatural.

The hardest part of infertility for me was never getting to grow my child in my womb, hold my child in my arms, see his first tooth, hear his first words, watch his first step, or take him to his first day of school.

The emotional pain went much deeper than that, as it included never seeing his graduation, wedding, or our first grandchild, and knowing the Hoffman name in our immediate family ended *here* with us. It was a gap so wide—more like a canyon that was not so grand. It hurt so bad, and sometimes still does, that I do not know why infertility even exists! But God does...

I am sharing all of this with you because I want you to know that I have been through many trials in my faith walk, as I am sure you have, too. I have lost not only children and grandchildren to infertility, but all of the experiences and memories that go with those relationships. Stage 4 lung cancer for nonsmoking women was not the first trial to enter my life, and quite honestly, I am sure it won't be the last.

Onward!

Trials are not easy, but God is faithful and He always causes us to triumph in Christ Jesus. He teaches His children how to overcome obstacles with faith in His Name. Through this refining process, we learn to please God. Pleasing God causes us to grow stronger in our faith, and become spiritually mature in our love for others. Our character is refined and we become more like Jesus when we face our trials with God and trust His outcome.

I have learned to overcome adversity through praise, worship, and pure faith in Jesus' Name. In the midst of the storm, God is faithful and sticks closer than a brother.

Receiving and Growing in the Call
A year after I received Christ, the Holy Spirit began ministering and speaking into my heart, "Preaching, preaching…" I kept hearing this word repeated to me every day for two years. You would think I would get the message, but I excused it by thinking to myself, *"God doesn't need me to preach. He has enough preachers!"* The irony of it is, at night, I dreamed of myself preaching and the Lord allowed me to hear myself preaching in my ear while I slept but I still remained in complete denial.

Finally, when my girlfriend Barb stepped up to receive her calling to preach, I went to hear her first pulpit message. Her faith and trust in God so inspired me that I went home that night and surrendered in a prayer, "Lord, if that is what You want me to do, I will do it!"

Instantly, I had total peace and called my pastor and told him what the Lord had put into my heart. He was in complete agreement and asked me if I wanted to speak at the monthly church prayer meetings. I accepted his offer and went on to not only teach at the monthly prayer meetings, but also ministered in elderly home services, wrote and taught many Bible studies, and visited and prayed with patients in hospital rooms.

When we moved to Florida, 14 years later, the Lord began redefining and aligning the ministry work He had given me to do, and He was increasing my calling to "pastor." This revelation was different from the initial call to preach because I always saw myself as an evangelist or a short-term missionary, not a pastor. Although I ministered and taught God's Word for years, while continuing to work in a corporate office setting and then a church office, God was now asking something different from me.

This is how the pastoral call happened—I was working long hours as a manager in a retail store on Sanibel Island. One morning, as I was driving across the causeway, I prayed, "Lord, I need Your encouragement, not a man, not a woman, I need YOU to encourage me." When I arrived at the store, I went to the back room. It was there that the Lord spoke to me while His power and presence came down all over me. I was engulfed in His presence (like Moses at the burning bush). In an indescribable way, He communicated a message of hope and encouragement by asking, "Do you know how gifted and talented you are to manage and administrate a business?" I was shocked! I wanted encouragement, but I was not expecting to hear that.

I then proceeded to the front of the store. I was now standing by a four-way clothing rack (before the store opened) and the power and presence of the Lord came down all over me again. He said, "If I can trust you with a store, I can trust you with a congregation." The thought of being a pastor came all over me. Then I walked to the back of the store to a dressing room. It had a small curtain in front of it. I was amazed at what I was experiencing.

I stepped into that small dressing room, which now became a prayer closet, and the presence and power of God came down all over me for the third time and the thought of being a pastor came to me again. I looked up to Heaven and said, "Lord, I am not worthy, but with Your help it would not be impossible." From there, I made an appointment to talk to my women's pastor who told me the steps I needed to take to facilitate credentials, so I would be ready to step into the places God called me to when the time was right.

After 4-5 years of working full-time, studying, taking online and district exams, and continuing to minister God's Word, I received my ordination credential from the General Council of the Assemblies of God at our district council meeting in May 2011. All praise to God!

My role as a minister is to love and lead people to Christ with the Gospel message and to help, inspire, and train believers to fulfill their callings. It is a blessing to write and teach my own Bible studies. Jeff and I have traveled to South Africa, Honduras, Portugal, and Romania on short-term missions trips. I have initiated and led corporate prayer services, mentored women, counseled, performed marriage ceremonies and celebration of life services, preached at Christian women's conferences, retreats, seminars, and other special events. And most of all, I have grown in my love, devotion, and worship of God. My goal is to keep the main thing (my relationship with God), the main thing according to Matthew 6:33, "But seek first the kingdom of God and His righteousness and all these things shall be added to you."

I am blessed to help encourage cancer patients, write devotionals and words of encouragement on social media, and have experienced the Person, power, and the presence of God in my daily life.

I prayed for the salvation of my husband, Jeff, for 17 years (neither of us were Christians when we married), and he has been saved for 16 years now—Praise God! Pray! Believe! Obey! Receive!

God answered YES to many of my prayers, NO to some, and WAIT on others. He has not given me everything I want, but He has been faithful to give me everything I need. He has left out nothing that would have been necessary in serving Him. He uses what I do not have to bring forth things that He alone can manifest.

I love God because He first loved me.

I now realize that a family of two, or should I say three—The Lord, Jeff, and me—is a complete family. There is nothing lacking in our lives because Christ is first and foremost and our union is complete in Him. A single person is complete in Christ—one is a whole number—I learned that long ago.

So you also are complete through your union with Christ,
who is the head over every ruler and authority.
Colossians 2:10 NLT

☙

There is no one who can take the Lord's place in our lives—not a man, woman, or child. Our relationship with God is the key to right living and every other relationship.

> *...And what does the Lord require of you but to do justly,*
> *to love mercy, and to walk humbly with your God?*
> Micah 6:8b
> ⌖

Now as we venture into the next phase of our journey, walking through cancer, Jeff and I needed to rely fully on all of our prior victories, God's faithfulness, and His promised present help. I will endeavor, as best as I can, to walk you through this unexpected trial of our faith. Let the healing begin…

THE COUGH
Chapter 1

What's Happening?

I began having a "little" cough in April 2015. At first, I did not think anything of it because I was seldom sick. In fact, I have been blessed to be healthy my entire life. Once or twice a year, I might get a cold, but nothing beyond that—my medical records were always clear…that is, until now.

By early May, however, this little cough became more nagging and consistent. It started showing up on a daily basis. I tried some over-the-counter remedies to no avail. It was then that I decided to consult with my family doctor to see if there was anything else I could do to get rid of the cough. When I called to make the appointment, it surprised me that the next opening was a month and a half away. I chose not to schedule that far in advance for something that seemed so minor. After all, it was probably just a sinus infection, right? Jeff and I were planning a short getaway trip in July to see our family in Pennsylvania. Surely, by that time, the cough would be long gone and it would not matter anymore.

July came and Jeff and I were in Pennsylvania, as planned. Can you guess who else decided to visit with us? Yes, the unwelcome cough!

My eldest sister, Debbie, had concerns that the presence of this cough potentially represented something far more serious. As we were taking a walk, I was coughing. Without hesitation she said, "I don't like the way that cough sounds! I hope it's not cancer!" Her candor shocked me, but I appreciated her honesty. "Cancer? Are you kidding me?? No way! I have been healthy my whole life. It's probably just a sinus infection. No worries. I will definitely make a doctor's appointment when I get back to Fort Myers." I kept that promise.

Fast forwarding a week or two, I had my appointment, and my doctor sent me immediately for a chest X-ray. When the films were read, the results were "CLEAR and NORMAL," but I kept coughing. After a few rounds of antibiotics that did not remedy the situation, my husband and I decided to switch doctors and get a second opinion. I was blessed to get one of the most wonderful primary care physicians I have ever had, Dr. Syed.

During my initial appointment with Dr. Syed, I stated the following concerns: rapid progression of the "little" cough that soon developed into a bigger cough, how unusual it was for me to be sick on any level, and the uncharacteristic length of time that this cough had been lingering (four months at this point).

Since my X-ray showed clear and normal, we decided to try a different type of medication, cough syrup, and a moist air heat facial sprayer. After the new prescriptions were finished, I was still coughing.

But why?

I remember laying on our couch at night, watching TV, and grasping at straws to try and figure out **why** I kept coughing. Never imagining it was anything serious.

I blamed it on the couch and kiddingly told my husband, "There must be something on this couch that's making me cough!" To which he responded, "No, honey, I sit on that same couch all the time and I never cough." He was right, of course, but surely it is not normal to cough all day for no reason. Finding THE solution became my top priority.

When I called the primary care office for another appointment, I explained the persisting cough, so they worked me right into their schedule. Then my doctor started to dig even deeper. He referred me to an ENT (ears, nose, and throat) specialist first. The ENT put a scope up my nose and down my throat—an unpleasant experience. (Thank God Jeff was in the room with me. I focused on him, instead of the bright light shining in my eyes and the thin tube that was snaking its way through my nose and into my throat.) I nearly gagged and could not wait to get out of there. No offense to the specialist, but I do not care for anything done around my face, including my eyes, nose, and mouth.

After seeing nothing out of the ordinary in my nose or throat, this specialist thought the cough would go away on its own, but it didn't.

Now keep in mind, I am not a go-to-the-doctor type of person. Number one, because I have enjoyed divine health my entire life, and number two, if I ever do catch a cold or something minor, it always goes away quickly and I am soon well again. BUT this time... it was extremely different. This little cough had grown into a bigger nonstop cough, and it was not going away either on its own, or with the prescriptions, and it was becoming a nuisance to me.

My new primary care doctor was so understanding, kind, caring, thorough, and definitely working on getting to the root of the problem. Knowing the severity of the cough, and wanting me to have relief, he gave me an open door to see him. "If you are not feeling well," he told me, "call the office anytime and I will make sure to fit you into the schedule." I took him up on that offer and went to see him a third time—this is contrary to my nature, but you have to know your body and listen to its symptoms. My body was saying, "Help me! I want to stop coughing!"

I became like a lion hunting its prey. I was in fierce pursuit of a solution and insistent on finding one. My doctor felt the same way. He explained to Jeff and me that his next specialist referral was a pulmonologist, and then, if needed, an allergist. He was so good at keeping the ball rolling... I was honestly glad to see anyone, at this point, to help me get better, and to permanently get rid of the ever-intensifying cough.

THE DOCTOR APPOINTMENTS
Chapter 2

What Is It?

Dr. Syed sent me to Dr. Challapalli (pulmonologist). Dr. Challapalli is a wonderful doctor. He also is thorough, kind, and caring. After prescribing stronger cough syrup, cough pills, and inhalers to help make me comfortable and alleviate the symptoms, he ordered an upper CT (Computerized Tomography) scan and a breathing test.

I am not sure if I completely failed the breathing test, but I know I struggled with it. I could not inhale enough air (using the breathing exerciser) to get the blue marker within the normal range numbers—it always fell far below that mark. It was taxing for me to take deep breaths without coughing. The person giving me the test thought I might have asthma… but I didn't.

Shortly after the upper CT scan was completed, Dr. Challapalli called me on my cell phone. It was after 5:00 p.m. on a week day and Jeff and I were on our way to dinner. I thought a call directly from a doctor after office hours was unusual, but when he told me that the CT scan showed that I had "spots," it made more sense to me. I knew "spots" did not sound good, but I withheld putting a whole lot of emphasis on it because we were still in the fact-gathering stage and only beginning to put the pieces of the puzzle together. Dr. C said that he did not know what "it" was, so he asked me to get a lower CT scan, as well.

The following week, I returned to the hospital to get the lower CT scan. The technician walked me to the changing room in the scan area and asked me to put on a hospital gown. When ready, I sat down on the sliding bed that would soon transport me into the "donut machine." This strange and new medical environment hit my heart hard. Out of nowhere warm tears began gently streaming down my cheeks.

I looked at the technician and confided in her as if she were a close friend, "They said I have spots on my lungs." Stopping to blow my nose, wipe the tears from my eyes, and compose myself, I continued, "I have been healthy my whole life!" She spoke no words, but looked at me with love and compassion, gave me a much needed hug, another tissue to pat my tears, and a loving smile. I felt extremely comforted in that moment and then into the machine I went.

Once inside the machine, a woman's voice (that sounds like she works at NASA space center) directed me to "take a deep breath and hold…" I have to be honest, it was challenging to hold my breath. I thought my cheeks would burst before I heard her next command, "Breathe…" What a relief! The recorded voice repeats the same instructions a few times before the technician injects the iodine contrast into the IV to make the image on the CT scan stand out. At that point, the tech advises, "You may feel a warm sensation, or have a copper taste." I experienced the warm sensation, but never the copper taste.

I tried my best to comply with the breathing instructions and to keep my cough low-key during the scan. I also did plenty of praying in that machine. Looking up to God (with my eyes closed), I prayed, "Lord, I need to be still so they get a good read on the scan. Please help me not to cough. Thank You, God, that You are with me through all of this. I give You praise and glory in Jesus' Name. Amen!"

When the lower CT scan was completed, my pulmonologist called me again, "Germaine, this is Dr. Challapalli. I received your CT results and I need you and your husband to come see me in my office immediately—TODAY—this afternoon." Of course, the urgency in his voice was concerning, but Jeff and I agreed to remain calm. We valued, respected, and trusted our doctor and his judgment. We were thankful that he took our case so seriously and dropped all other plans for the day. Seeing Dr. Challapalli was our sole priority.

When we arrived in his office, midafternoon, as requested, he let us know it was his day off, but that our appointment was of paramount importance to him and "the right way to do things." He wanted to talk to us face to face, not over the phone. Dr. C was straightforward. He explained that the upper CT scan showed "innumerable spots" on my lungs, so many they could not count them all… WHAT??

And my lower CT scan showed that I had a tumor on my right ovary. DOUBLE WHAT??

He proceeded to tell us, "You need surgery to remove the tumor right away! I have already arranged it. I called a wonderful gynecologic oncologist, Dr. Sandadi. He will take care of you." WOW! That was a lot to digest in one sitting.

When Jeff and I visited with Dr. Sandadi, he explained further that the tumor was the size of a baseball and showed us the CT scan image on his computer.

After we viewed the scan, all three of us gathered at a small round table in his office to discuss the procedure to remove the tumor. He gave us a few options and we chose to have the surgery right away.

I thank God that Dr. Challapalli sent me for the lower CT scan because I would have never known that I had a tumor. I never had any symptoms… no pain, no discomfort, no side effects, nothing!

THE DIAGNOSIS
Chapter 3

What? How Can This Be?

On November 10, 2015, I went into the hospital to have the tumor on my right ovary removed. I will NEVER forget that date because it is my mother's birthday. She, Adelaide, lovingly known as "Del," and my father, Jerry, have been in Heaven for over 15 years—they never saw my 40th birthday. They went to Heaven after 46 years of marriage, six months apart from each other. I miss them dearly and look forward to being reunited with them again one day in Glory.

Before the surgery, Dr. Sandadi explained to us that the extent of surgery would be determined by what he found first through the laparoscopic procedure. He also was caring, concerned, and kind. We were blessed to have the best doctors and nurses working with us and for us. God handpicked a circle of excellence to take care of me, His little girl.

Immediately following the surgery, Dr. Sandadi updated my husband on my condition. The surgery, indeed, became more extensive and he performed a full hysterectomy (complete with 37 staples). He also gave Jeff the best news we could have hoped for—the tumor was benign! Hallelujah! There were prior suspicions that the tumor may have been the source of the problem emanating up into my lungs, but the fact that the tumor was benign ruled that out. Thank God!

A couple days later, I was scheduled to have a lung biopsy due to my "innumerable spots." The hospital pulmonologist was all set to take samples of both of my lungs. Right before anesthesia, a nurse (or an angel) came and whispered in my ear, "Jesus is with you. Jesus is in the room. Jesus is with you!" I fell asleep right after I heard that, so comforted with God's peace.

After the biopsy was completed, the pulmonologist came into our hospital room to talk with Jeff and me. He told us that the samples showed that it was cancer—**non-small cell lung cancer for nonsmoking women**... Huh? Is he talking to me??? Non-small cell what? For nonsmoking women? I didn't even know there was such a thing.

I was in a state of shock and disbelief. All of the bells and whistles were going off in my head. *"I have cancer for not smoking? Really?"* Jeff asked the doctor how far along it was and he said, "Since it is in both lungs, it is stage 4. BUT," he confidently continued, "God can heal you, and I will pray that God heals you!"

God knows what you need and when you need it. I definitely needed to hear my doctor's words of faith and compassion—they anchored my resolve, stirred my spirit, and provided unwavering hope for my future. It was another God moment and music to my ears, but the news itself was not anything that I was expecting.

Everything felt surreal.

Jeff and I looked at each other, got into bed, held each other close and cried. What else could we do? Jeff said to me, "I have loved you for 34 years and I want 30 more..." Me too, my husband, me too...

OUR FAITH JOURNEY
Chapter 4

Walking Through the Process

Following the initial diagnosis, walking out the next few months became physically grueling, but spiritually, my faith remained strong. Jeff and I decided from the "get-go" that we would both stay positive. If one of us would get slightly off track, the other one would be sure to steer the other back onto the faith track—and it worked.

When I was released from the hospital, after having the tumor removed, the hysterectomy, the initial lung cancer diagnosis, and later learning this type of cancer has a less than 1% survival rate, Dr. Challapalli confirmed that the best thing I could do was to maintain a positive attitude. He then told me, "The way you are going through this is awesome. I have never seen such a positive attitude as yours!" Hallelujah! All glory to God!

I can honestly say—Jesus made ALL of the difference! He gave me the gift of His peace. Philippians 4:7 speaks of it, **"and the peace of God, which surpasses all understanding, will guard your hearts and minds through Christ Jesus."** I am a living example that this particular Bible promise was not written on an ancient scroll for only those who walked with God long ago. But, as it is with all of the other promises found in God's Word, it was a right now, available, on-time "rhema" Word (rhema is the portion of Scripture that speaks to a believer—refers to a current situation or need). Jesus, the Living Word, gave life to His written Word.

I experienced, firsthand, the power of God's presence and His mighty love. His ABIDING GRACE and PERFECT PEACE partnered to give me the courage to move forward morning, noon, and night—no matter what trial I had to face. The Prince of Peace, the Lord Jesus Christ, lovingly extended His Heavenly scepter to Jeff and me.

He walked through the entire process with us like a parent taking their child to school for the first time and making sure they made it to their classroom, met their teacher, assimilated with classmates, and received the necessary books and supplies to take their classes. The class we were enrolled in was called, "Walking Through Cancer." Our supplies included the Word of God, faith, and prayer. Our Teacher was the Holy Spirit, and our classmates were everyone on this globe who prayed with us and for us around the clock. The incredible medical team and staff that took care of me played a vital role in our outcome, as well.

Jeff became my loving, constant caretaker, observing and noting every symptom. Without any complaint, he helped me through months of nonstop coughing, daily low grade fevers, multiple blood draws, joint pain, low oxygen levels, doctor's visits, and trips on hospital gurneys (for procedures and surgery). He watched me prep for CT scans, helped me take off and put on my post-op compression boots, and assisted me while I walked in excruciating pain with 37 staples intact and an IV pole trailing behind me—he was so faithful, devoted, and strong. I drew from his faith and strength, as he drew from mine.

Later in the process he told me, "I learned something about you, Babe. You are fragile on the outside, but you are strong on the inside." All glory to God!

I know that the strength he was referring to was not my personal strength, but God's strength in me. The Lord promises in His Word that He will never leave nor forsake us, and He kept that promise. My close relationship with God and His proven faithfulness in my life helped me to trust His perfect plan, no matter what the outcome. I believed everything was working together for the good—whether or not I saw it or felt it.

This Scripture strengthened and encouraged me:

And we know that all things work together for good to those who love God, to those who are the called according to His purpose.
Romans 8:28
🕊

I learned that all things are NOT good, but **all things do work together** for the good. And I stood on that promise!

The Lord taught me a few simple, but amazing spiritual lessons that helped me dramatically and increased my faith. I pray that they increase yours, too!

SPIRITUAL LESSONS:
1. **The Lord didn't shut the mouths of the lions UNTIL Daniel was in the lions' den.** (Notice that was plural—there was more than one lion in that den.) Daniel 6:18-23, "Now the king went to his palace and spent the night fasting; and no musicians were brought before him. Also his sleep went from him. [19] Then the king arose very early in the morning and went in haste to the den of lions. [20] And when he came to the den, he cried out with a lamenting voice to Daniel. The king spoke, saying to Daniel, 'Daniel, servant of the living God, has your God, whom you serve continually, been able to deliver you from the lions?' [21] Then Daniel said to the king, 'O king, live forever! [22] **My God sent His angel and shut the lions' mouths, so that they have not hurt me, because I was found innocent before Him;** and also, O king, I have done no wrong before you.' [23] Now the king was exceedingly glad for him, and commanded that they should take Daniel up out of the den. So Daniel was taken up out of the den, and no injury whatever was found on him, because he believed in his God."

2. **The Lord didn't take the heat out of the fire UNTIL Shadrach, Meshach, and Abed-Nego were thrown into the fiery furnace.** After these three young men refused to worship the gods Nebuchadnezzar made and the gold image he set up, he had them thrown into a fiery furnace that was **heated seven**

times more than usual and the flame of the fire killed the men who took up Shadrach, Meshach, and Abed-Nego. Daniel 3:14-30 contains the full account, but I want to focus on verses 24-25, "Then King Nebuchadnezzar was astonished; and he rose in haste and spoke, saying to his counselors, 'Did we not cast three men bound (*and fully clothed*—parenthetical and italics mine) into the midst of the fire?' " They answered and said to the king, 'True, O king.' ²⁵ 'Look!' he answered, **'I see four men loose, walking in the midst of the fire; and they are not hurt, and the form of the fourth is like the Son of God.' "** Then the king called for the young men to come out of the fire and they were **untouched and unharmed.** Their hair was not singed and their clothes did not smell. The king decreed anyone who spoke against their God would be cut in pieces. Verses 29b-30 proclaim, " '…there is no other God who can deliver like this.'³⁰Then the king promoted Shadrach, Meshach, and Abed-Nego in the province of Babylon."

3. **The Lord didn't part the Jordan River UNTIL the priests stepped down into it by faith.** Joshua 3:13-17, " 'And it shall come to pass, as soon as the soles of the feet of the priests who bear the ark of the Lord, the Lord of all the earth, shall rest in the waters of the Jordan, that the waters of the Jordan shall be cut off, the waters that come down from upstream, and they shall stand up as a heap.' ¹⁴ So it was, when the people set out from their camp to cross over the Jordan, with the priests bearing the ark of the covenant before the people, ¹⁵ and as those who bore the ark came to the Jordan, and the feet of the priests who bore the ark dipped in the edge of the water (for the Jordan overflows all its banks during the whole time of harvest), ¹⁶ that the waters which came down from upstream stood still, and rose in a heap very far away at Adam, the city that is beside Zaretan. So the waters that went down into the Sea of Arabah, the Salt Sea, failed, and were cut off; and the people crossed over opposite Jericho. ¹⁷ **Then the priests who bore the ark of the covenant of the Lord stood firm on dry ground in the midst of the Jordan; and all Israel crossed over on dry ground,** until all the people had crossed completely over the Jordan." Amazing!

While I was pondering how best to help others with cancer, the Lord spoke to me in a very loving Father-daughter way—

> He said, **"There are cancers worse than the physical ones.** Cancers of the mind, heart, and attitudes. Cancers of unbelief, doubt, and fear that spread among God's people. Cancers of sin and darkness that destroy relationships, homes, and marriages. Inner thoughts that are not focused on God that leave people feeling hopeless, rejected, and unwanted [are cancerous]. From the wealthiest business people, to the poorest people, the struggle remains."

I took notes as fast as I could. The steady flow of wisdom that poured forth from my Heavenly Father's mouth to my heart was like healing living water sent from Heaven. There is a divine order to everything. The simple truth is, God wants us to have faith in Him, and to **USE** the faith we have. Sooner or later, our faith will be put to the test. If you have faith in God, even the size of a tiny mustard seed, it is enough. **One speck of faith activated by the Holy Spirit and used by the believer is more powerful than a truckload of doubt and fear.** Yes, Jesus taught us faith the size of a mustard seed is enough to speak to the mountain in our lives and command it to move and it will obey (Matthew 17:20). Jeff and I planned on using our mustard seeds!

We serve a God of miracles who requires faith.

> *But without faith it is impossible to please Him,*
> *for he who comes to God must believe that He is, and that*
> *He is a rewarder of those who diligently seek Him.*
> Hebrews 11:6
> ❧

Jeff and I could never have gone through this walk through cancer without God. He cushioned every blow, softened every trial, took the heat out of the fire, and shut the mouths of lions. Like the Israelites who stepped down into the Jordan River by faith in God, many years before us, we truly walked through the sea of cancer—equipped with God's grace, faith, and strength—as on dry land.

Every time Jeff and I should have or could have been knocked over by a wave of negative reports, the Lord reached down His Mighty Hand and lifted us higher. He enabled us to walk by faith, not by sight, in the midst of our circumstances. **Knowing the Lord's character and faithfulness became an immovable and impenetrable fortress round about us!** We were safe in the hands of God and no man could pluck us out. As Romans 8:31b asks, "...If God be for us, who can be against us?" God definitely was for us every step of the way!

GOD'S INSTRUCTION
Chapter 5

"Stretch Out Your Hand!"

I want to share some of the wonderful words of my husband with you because he was a major part of my healing process. He was always so positive and uplifting. When I was spending many hours a day on the couch in our living room, I would say to him, "Honey, I want to be able to get up off this couch and have some energy." And he would answer, "You will!" I would also say, "Honey, I want to walk up the steps again, pain free!" And his response was, "You will!" Or, I would open my heart and express, "I want to feel like myself again!" And he gently and lovingly reassured me, "You will!" His positive reinforcement was truly a great strength to me and it helped me to stay on top of the situation instead of falling headlong into it. My goal for 2016 was to be cough free, pain free, and cancer free.

WORDS FROM MY HUSBAND
Be Blessed by Jeff's Words of Faith…
On November 12, 2015, the doctor came into our hospital room after examining the lung biopsy report and gave us the terrible news. He told us my wife had stage 4 lung cancer for nonsmoking women. Seconds later he added, "God CAN heal you!"

Afterwards, I crawled into the hospital bed with my girl and we cried together in disbelief about what we just heard.

After we both fell asleep, GOD awoke me at 3:00 a.m. He spoke powerfully, clearly, and directly into my heart, "Stretch out your hand and I will heal her," so I did. What a powerful moment with my Heavenly Father. He was in the midst of this fiery trial with us. He knew what I could bear and how far He could take me. He also knew what my wife could bear. His intervention in this hour of greatest need showed Himself strong on our behalf. God was working!

He was also lifting me by the power of His love, speaking an instruction of faith, and giving me a promise that He would heal her. He was not off on some distant cloud somewhere unaware. He was right there in our hospital room, by my side, and at my wife's bedside. He was speaking truth and life to me about healing my girl. It doesn't get any more personal than that. This encounter with God became my cornerstone and point of reference for me to have faith in Him alone and not what I would see or hear in the months to come from all of the negative doctor's reports and medical research.

One of the nurses recommended that I educate myself on non-small cell cancer, so I did. She encouraged me and said, "Read all you can and gain all the knowledge necessary." The more I read, studied, and learned, the grimmer things looked. I kept all of this to myself—only sharing some of the details with immediate family members. I never told my wife anything that I learned about the cancer, and its potential progression, knowing this would not help her at all.

However, watching her endure test after test, including a needle biopsy through her back into her lungs, the different symptoms arising, and the horrible cough persisting, the medical knowledge I had obtained from all of the research, made the whole process more difficult for me. I told myself and our family siblings many times that I would do everything humanly possible to help her, but in the end, God had to step in and heal her 100%.

My bride endured many kinds of tests and procedures ranging from EKG's, PET, and CT scans to blood tests, biopsies, and chemo treatments—plus major side effects. I was by her side for all of it and I told her that I was keeping my vows, "in sickness and in health," and I meant it.

I remember a few times, right before bedtime, after I just finished praying for the cough to stop that a couple minutes later she would start coughing again. It was so disheartening because I knew the incredible pain that she was in and how much it hurt her chest and throat when she coughed. I prayed out loud, in some degree of frustration, because I felt that my prayer was not being answered. Other than those few moments, I always kept a good composure. After all, she needed my full support and positive influence. We both decided very early on to always stay on the positive road and never go down the negative road. There were only a handful of times that we moved off course, but always encouraged the other to get back on the positive road. I tried to do everything a good, godly husband should do—I listened to her, prayed for her and with her, stayed by her side, and encouraged her every day!

As we continued praying in the evenings together, I always prayed for the seen and the unseen. While we could see different things improving like the cough finally diminishing, rash clearing, swelling going down in her feet and legs, pain leaving her body, we could never see what was happening inside of her lungs. This is where FAITH has always been the most important part of our journey.

Stretch out your hand with healing power; may miraculous signs and wonders be done through the name of your holy servant Jesus.
Acts 4:30 NLT

What a loving Heavenly Father we have. He still does miracles on our behalf when we ask in faith in Jesus' Name and believe Him for the outcome. This is a promise we both chose to stand on. It is amazing how God's simple, yet profound instruction to me, "Stretch out your hand and I will heal her," was streamlined and paralleled with His written Word in the book of Acts.

❖

Amen, my wonderful husband! Part of the healing promise includes walking by faith. God will always do His part; we have to do our part. When we can't physically see the way through, we can always pray and praise our way through. We serve the God of all flesh and there is NOTHING too hard for Him (Jeremiah 32:27). There is no sickness or disease He cannot heal—that includes cancer!

Bless the Lord, O my soul; and all that is within me, bless His holy name! ²Bless the Lord, O my soul; and forget not all His benefits: ³ Who forgives all your iniquities, Who heals all your diseases…
Psalm 103:1-3

*But Jesus looked at them and said,
"With men it is impossible, but not with God;
for with God all things are possible."*
Mark 10:27

I just believed!

ONCOLOGY
A NEW WORD FOR US
Chapter 6

Walking Through Cancer

Meeting Our Oncologist
I was referred to a wonderful oncologist, Dr. Harwin. He is an expert in his field and came highly recommended. He is a mountain mover who sees the possibilities in hopeless situations, takes action, and gets results. Jeff and I highly respect and appreciate him.

Due to the critical stage 4 condition of my case and urgent need to act, Dr. Harwin began having my blood tested in his lab. He also sent my lung biopsy samples to Europe and a few other parts of the United States for testing and analysis.

I was not a "typical" case. Test results confirmed that I had two different types of mutations (a mutation occurs when a DNA gene is damaged or changed in such a way as to alter the genetic message carried by that gene). The good news, and relief for us, came when we learned that due to the mutations, I did not qualify at that time for standard chemo treatments or the clinical trials. That was a relief because everything we were now experiencing was still so new and I was not ready to extend my arm (or emotionally extend my heart) for chemotherapy treatments and did not want to be a part of a trial. Trial, to me, meant experiment (although I realize trials are necessary to find new and improved treatments).

Up to this point, I had very limited knowledge about the whole cancer process. Jeff and I were not ruling out whatever was necessary for treatment, but we were **extremely happy** not to commit to it up front. Plus, we wanted to get a second opinion from another cancer center. Our second opinion confirmed that we were headed on the right track and taking the best course of action.

In lieu of standard chemotherapy, I began taking a chemo pill in December 2015. I was thankful not to be getting regular chemo treatments, but a month or so later, began developing major side effects from the drug and continued having unexplainable low-grade fevers every day. I dehydrated, losing 26 pounds in two months, and lost my appetite. I ate a small amount at a time—not a regular portion—and after only a few bites my stomach would start churning. It became a rare occasion for me to be able to finish eating a meal without needing to run to the bathroom—this side effect wasted all of the nutrition I was trying to take in.

Nutrition
Due to the dehydration and sudden weight loss, Jeff and I went to see a nutritionist who was based in a medical services building. We needed a food plan to try to fatten me up a bit. As Jeff and I were rounding the corner through the hall to her office, out of the corner of my eye, I could see people in big green recliner chairs hooked up to their IV chemo treatments.

I admit it made me feel queasy to even think about the multitudes of people around the world who are going through the cancer treatment process, tucked away in quiet corners, with utter dependence on beating the odds through technology and medical advancements, fearing the unknown, and trying to make sense of it all.

As human beings, we all have our limitations—whether in knowledge, talent, or decision-making. I began seeing the silhouette of those limitations in the faces of men and women who were now hooked up to IV poles and receiving their chemo treatments. Their frail and courageous images were now permanently embedded in my mind and heart. Once you see the reality of those weakened bodies, bald heads, and bruised veins, you can't unsee it. And I was becoming part of that reality.

Let's face it, cancer is a shocking and heavy weight that lands squarely on our shoulders and demands our attention. Thankfully, we do not have to carry that burden alone.

God is our place of refuge and strength. He is our source of peace and safety. We can release every worry, doubt, fear, and concern to Him. 1 Peter 5:7 shows us the way, "Casting all your care upon Him (God), for He cares for you.

On our way home from my appointment at the nutritionist, the Lord spoke a life-changing word to me while stopped at a traffic light. He said, "I want you to help people with cancer." A bit puzzled by His request (which seemed so far beyond me) I paused, "You do? …Ok, with Your help, Lord, I will." I had no idea what exactly the Lord was planning, but I knew it would be good. All of God's plans are good, fair, and just. He was giving me a front row seat to understanding cancer by allowing me to walk through it.

Believers know there is so much more than hi-tech knowledge and medical advancements that beats cancer—but they, too, have struggles. I am reminded of Jesus in the Garden of Gethsemane, the Son of God, who was praying and laying His life down for us, Luke 22:44 says, "And being in agony, He prayed more earnestly. Then His sweat became like great drops of blood falling down to the ground."

There is no sin in the struggle.

Although I am truly grateful for technology, medical advancements, and new treatments (they have helped me greatly), I know they can only take us so far. God and our faith in His great abilities to heal our mind, body, soul, and spirit have to take us the rest of the way. There are many people in treatment chairs who have faith, but they also have questions and concerns about their healing process. How long will this last? Will I get better? Am I doing things the right way? Among many others… God understands what we are going through and He gives us the power to endure. When we pray, God answers.

Hebrews 4:16 says, "Let us therefore come boldly to the throne of grace, that we may **obtain mercy** and **find grace** to help in time of need." God created the Heavens and the Earth, and you and me. He will be faithful to provide the right people and resources at the right time to lead and guide us on our journey. He knows we struggle when faced with adversity, and He offers His healing hand of hope and faith.

Allow me to reiterate, there is no sin in the struggle. I have yet to meet one person who did not struggle with a cancer diagnosis.

Who's In Control?
One of the greatest challenges a cancer patient can face, however, often occurs when we are **unwilling** to let go of the struggle because we want to be in control. And, we see control slipping away. There is an unhealthy dose of control and there is healthy dose of control.

Unhealthy Control
When we feel helpless and hopeless, even defeated by cancer, we can try to control our circumstances and outcome by storming around on the inside in utter frustration. We can become negative in our own thinking. And we can begin to lash out at God, family, friends, doctors, nurses, or others who are trying to help us. Why do we do this? I believe it is our fear of the unknown.

We can't see an immediate result or an end to our malady, so we imagine the worst possible outcome instead of the best. Progressively, as our bodies weaken and our white blood counts, hemoglobin, or platelet levels drop, negative thoughts infiltrate our peaceful thinking. Gradually, we can find ourselves coming into agreement with our darkest fears, and wonder, *"Am I going to make it?"*

Healthy Control
When we surrender our will and outcome to God, on the other hand, we choose as Jesus did, to **relinquish control and trust God's wisdom**—at that moment, we win! **Peace replaces fear and faith replaces doubt.** It is only through the humble prayer of surrender, "Not my will, Lord, but Yours be done," that we begin healing and trusting someone other than ourselves—someone stronger than ourselves—someone who is so much greater than ourselves—someone

who loves us with an everlasting love—**His Name is God Almighty**. Giving Him control of our lives and outcome allows us to walk in the spirit of freedom, peace, and self-control.

Self-Control—A Fruit of the Holy Spirit
God never gave us control over circumstances or one another. He did, however, give us the ability to use the fruit of the Holy Spirit called, **self-control**. This fruit is produced in us by abiding in Jesus. He, the Holy Spirit, enables us to **make right choices** and **maintain healthy attitudes** in our thinking, saying, and doing.

> *But the Holy Spirit produces this kind of fruit in our lives:*
> *love, joy, peace, patience, kindness, goodness,*
> *faithfulness, 23 gentleness, self-control.*
> Galatians 5:22-23a NLT

By giving our will to God, CANCER and its terrible taunts are captured and defeated. We now walk in the Spirit and have dominion over the voice of the enemy who insists, "You are not going to make it. Give up! You are going to die!" Lies. Lies. Lies. The devil is defeated, God is exalted, and Jesus is Lord.

Choose Life
Loving God, others, and ourselves is a choice. We CHOOSE LIFE!

> *I call Heaven and earth as witnesses today against you, that I have set*
> *before you life and death, blessing and cursing; therefore*
> *choose life, that both you and your descendants may live.*
> Deuteronomy 30:19

God created our bodies and He knows exactly how to heal them. He uses medicine and excellent doctors, and He also performs miracles, signs, and wonders. He is the Great Physician! We can put all of our faith and trust IN HIM.

> *Trust in the Lord with all your heart, and lean not on your own*
> *understanding; 6 In all your ways **acknowledge Him**,*
> *and He shall direct your paths.*
> Proverbs 3:5-6

Proverbs 3:6 gives us two key words to think on "acknowledge Him." To acknowledge is to accept or admit the existence or truth of. When we acknowledge that God is with us, we can sense His presence: If we deny His existence—we remain empty.

When you are face to face with someone you love, isn't it natural to expect that person to acknowledge you? God presents Himself to us by His Spirit, His Word, His people and all creation (Romans 1:20). It's up to us to acknowledge—accept—by faith that He is with us.

Chemo Pill
In the midst of taking the chemo pill, my body was feeling weaker, the cough seemed to be getting stronger, and I definitely was in need of a miracle! I had now been coughing daily—morning until night—for more than nine months—even though I took a cough pill several times a day. I woke up coughing in the middle of the night. I coughed like a heavy smoker, when I have **never smoked** in my life.

Every morning, the first 10 minutes of my day were spent coughing, gagging, and spitting up clear mucus. Sometimes I coughed until I cried. My fractured ribs will attest to it.

By the end of each day, a small trash can beside my sofa was overflowing with tissues from the cough! Jeff began purchasing the family-size, 4-pack, tissue boxes that I easily *blew* through in a week.

My chest hurt, my throat hurt, and talking for more than a few minutes aggravated the cough and weakened my voice. I avoided coughing fits by limiting and excusing myself from longer conversations. The weakened voice was challenging and a bit scary, too, because I have always been a verbal person. When my voice was at its weakest, laughing, singing, or any sustained talking was out of the question. One doctor told me that I would probably NEVER get my normal voice back...but I did!

As a side effect of the chemo drug, I developed an intense rash all over my body (except my face). Most people using this drug developed the rash on their face, too, but God spared me. The rash came with a horrendous itch. The skin on my legs flaked off and the surface area was raw, tender, and ready to bleed. Horrible! I used a topical cream, but the itch became so intolerable that I had no choice but to go see Dr. Harwin again.

The second he entered the exam room, I elevated my leg and pointed to the bright red splotches and pleaded, "Dr. Harwin, help me!" I felt like a small child who just fell off her bike at the playground. After taking one look at my red, swollen, irritated legs and feet, he took me off the cancer pill for a week and prescribed an antibiotic to clear up the rash and the itch. Thank God!

Multiple Blood Clots and Pulmonary Embolism
In addition to the rash and other side effects of the chemo drug, I developed multiple blood clots in my legs and a massive pulmonary embolism in my lungs.

Jeff and I were at a local mall trying to get some simple exercise—walking. The longer we walked through the mall, the more my left leg was hurting. It was not only hurting, it was swelling. The calf muscle was tightening and it became more and more agonizing to walk. I stopped several times to lean against a store front to take the pressure off of my leg. Since it was not getting any better, we decided to sit down on a bench at the end of the mall and rest awhile. Now this mall is relatively small and does not take more than five minutes to get from one end to the other, but this walk we were taking felt like a trek through the Sahara desert with no oasis in sight...

What is going on?

This whole process became more and more surreal.

Was I living in a nightmare?

My husband called Dr. Harwin the next day who told us to go to the emergency room. (I do not know why we waited a day, but we did.) It was still painful for me to walk, so after filling out all of the medical forms, the hospital admissions woman asked, "Do you think you can walk to your room?" I hesitated, "How far is it?" To which she countered, "With your answer, I will get the wheelchair. If you need to ask, 'How far?' that tells me that you need it."

I was wheeled to my room and soon taken to the ultrasound area. The technician applied the gel and rubbed the transducer over my legs. It was only moments until he discovered the multiple blood clots.

When the ultrasound was completed, I was wheeled down the hall to the CT scan room. As daunting as it was, I had to help scoot myself onto the bed of the "donut machine." The CT scan revealed the massive pulmonary embolism in my lungs. I was expeditiously moved to the Intensive Care Unit. Later, I learned the reason I was sent to the ICU was in case of an "event"—the potential event was 99% of the people who had what I had do not make it, and they did not think I would either... BUT GOD!

The small ICU room was cold—a brisk 50° because they were trying to break my fever. I felt badly as I looked over at Jeff from my petite, elevated bed (I felt like a baby in a crib). He was sitting in a chair directly across from me with a blanket up over his head trying to keep warm. I was so weak, the staff brought the X-ray machine into my ICU room to take pictures of my lungs. They also came later to do an ultrasound on my heart (which was perfect). I never had medical machinery coming to me like I did that night. But thank God, I made it to the next morning and the morning after that... Thank God! This was my FIRST MIRACLE—making it past the pulmonary embolism!

We spent another full week in the hospital. Jeff stayed with me the whole time. He slept in the recliner chair beside my bed. During this hospital stay, I had more blood drawn than I want to think about. I did not think there was another place they could find to poke me with a needle. Edema fluid developed in my legs and feet due to the blood clots. My feet were sore and swollen. To give you an idea of how swollen they were, I take a size 7.5 shoe and could not fit into a size 10. I wore slippers everywhere I went until Jeff found me two new pair of sandals with Velcro straps, which made it easier for me to slip in and out of, and allowed extra room for my now extra-wide feet.

The hospital doctors thought it would probably take 3-5 weeks for the swelling to go down, and it turned out to be five months later when my legs and feet went back to normal. As part of my morning routine, I lifted my legs to see if they looked normal... Not yet? Maybe tomorrow…

Because of the pain and swelling in my legs and feet, my husband was prepared to dismantle our bed and bring it downstairs to help avoid overexerting myself on the steps. But a nurse who formerly worked in home health care told us, "She can sit down on the steps and scoot up the stairs backwards." We followed her suggestion—even though at times, it took me a half an hour to do so. I still needed a walker to steady myself and get around on the first floor. Each night I felt like I was scaling Mount Everest. The second floor seemed so far away and all I wanted to do was to walk on my own two feet again—pain free!

When my friend Tara visited me from Pennsylvania, I watched in awe and wonder as she seemed to glide right up the stairs as if on an escalator to go to our guest bedroom. "WOW! I want to do that, too," I told her. "You will, honey, you will. Next time I come to visit, you will be walking on the beach with me." And guess what? It happened!

To prevent potential blood clots from forming in the future, a blood thinner injection was prescribed. A hospital nurse showed Jeff how to inject the needle into my stomach, so he could easily do it at home. He followed this procedure every day for 10 months. Ugh! I did not like that shot! The needle was thicker than I was used to. And, although it took only seconds to administer, I closed my eyes, grit my teeth, and braced myself because the injection hurt and caused minor bruising in my stomach. After each shot I reminded myself, *"It's only temporary!"* And, above all, I would rather have a daily injection than another blood clot!

In addition to the blood clot situation, I was still dealing with the aftermath of the rash. The skin on my legs, feet, and back dried out and it now began peeling off in thin sheer layers (the same way your skin peels as a result of sunburn). It took about two weeks until I was done "shedding" the old skin and new healthy skin was coming back.

My primary care physician made a request to the department of transportation to get a handicap parking status for me due to the swelling in my feet, the major joint pain, the lung cancer, constant cough, and breathing issues. I told him that I only wanted the *temporary* permit (versus the permanent) to hang on my visor because I did not plan on staying in this condition.

Jeff did all of the driving during that time, but we still needed the permit because I could not walk from point A to point B without getting out of breath. I wanted to have the freedom to drive again and was hoping it would be sooner rather than later. Praise God my temporary six-month handicap tag has long since expired.

New Treatment
Since continuing the chemo pill with all of its negative side effects was now out of the question, Jeff asked Dr. Harwin, "With chemo, can she beat this?" His highly-valued and much-needed "YES!" gave us the confidence to move forward. We immediately began to take the standard chemotherapy treatments. Initially, we expected only four rounds, but I ended up needing six full rounds of treatment.

I did not know quite what to expect or how I would feel getting the actual IV chemo treatments—although I was now officially a cancer patient. I was still in a state of shock and disbelief. Everything continued to feel surreal. It was as though I was in a God bubble—I was not in control, but He was, and I was going along for the ride. Being able to trust the Lord to take me through this process encouraged and comforted me.

In preparation for the first treatment, a wonderful oncology nurse explained some of the physical issues we could expect such as: fatigue, low blood counts, and low energy levels. She also promoted good nutrition, dental hygiene, lots of rest, and gave us literature to read on chemotherapy. She encouraged me to listen to my body in order to maintain the highest and best level of health. I appreciated her loving, gentle, and caring spirit.

I needed other medications prior to my new treatment: anti-nausea pills, a daily dose of folic acid, a steroid the day before, the day of, and the day after treatment to boost my energy level, and a vitamin B_{12} shot every nine weeks.

The staff at the cancer center was so good to us. I am thankful for them, and especially our team leader, Dr. Harwin, who helped pioneer the way for my miracle with his wealth of knowledge in cancer treatment. He always gave us top priority and made himself available to answer any questions.

The process for my treatment days entailed:
- Signing in at the front desk (Jeff always did this for me)
- Receiving my patient wristband
- Waiting to be called to the lab area
- Being asked my birthdate
- Walking to the lab area
- Stepping onto the scale
- Having vitals taken
- Being asked my birthdate again
- Drawing blood for a CBC (complete blood count)
- Sending the results directly to my doctor's computer
- Getting into the exam room
- Meeting with my oncologist.

After reviewing the bloodwork results with us, completing the physical exam, and discussing how to go forward, Dr. Harwin always walked Jeff and me back to the infusion room. Such a personal touch!

Infusion Room
When arriving at the infusion room for the first time, I felt shocked and out of sorts. It was like being invited to a secret room few people knew about. The experience was surreal—looking at the big recliners, IV poles, and the people in waiting chairs—it was real, but not registering in my brain.

A basket filled with donated hand-knit hats was always available on the nurses' counter for anyone who needed them (free of charge). A small bell with BIG meaning resided on a column near the counter. Inscribed on it, a sign of success, **Done-with-Chemo!** (Now that was something to look forward to!)

I met the nicest team of nurses who became friends and caregivers. When it was my turn to get set up for chemo, I extended my arm and the nurse inserted the IV needle, flushed it, and gauze taped it to my arm. I then proceeded to a comfortable recliner chair and waited for the pharmacy to mix up my chemo bags.

Every person has an individual mix for their particular type of cancer, and every person responds differently to the various side effects that accompany chemotherapy. Dr. Harwin did a great job in shoring up my medications to avoid nausea. Hallelujah!

It was a blessing that my husband, friends, and family members were always permitted to be with me during treatment, as long as seating was available. I was thankful to have Jeff, my friend Lisa (who kindly brought me lunch and a gift on all six treatment days), and a family member who flew in from Pennsylvania. If there was not enough room on any given day, two people rotated being by my side. My sister Eileen, nieces Jessie and Julie, and my friend Tara all came to at least one of my treatments. Being surrounded by those who love, pray, and believe with you is priceless. It meant the world to me.

My chemo regimen began by taking two anti-nausea pills that my husband brought from the pharmacy to give to the nurse, who in turn gave them to me. This was followed by an anti-nausea IV, and three different types of chemo. (I usually slept during chemo for an hour or two—I always brought slippers, a snuggly blankie, and wore comfortable clothes.) My regimen ended with a small medication patch being adhered to my arm to help boost my white blood count. After the needle snapped into my skin, like a bee sting, the medication dispersed within 24 hours. The device indicated when it was ready to be removed by a flashing light and a soft beep. My entire chemotherapy process could take five to six hours depending on how many patients needed attention that day.

God Is in the Details
A sweet sidebar: Have you ever had a craving for a favorite treat or snack that you enjoy? Think of it right now. What is your favorite snack? One of mine is chocolate chip cookies. Once, when I went for treatment, I had been wanting a chocolate chip cookie for days, but

never got it, so I prayed for it! During treatment, I was staring out the window when one of the nurses came beside me and presented me with a giant chocolate chip cookie on a plate and said, "In your honor!" I was shocked and elated. God cares about the details, even the smallest desires of our hearts, like chocolate chip cookies!

Gentle Boldness
During this walk through cancer, God birthed a new gentle boldness within me. I have always been a people-person who genuinely cares about others. If anyone shared a need with me, I always asked, "Can I pray with you about that?" The majority of the time, they answered, "YES!" I can count on one hand the times someone answered, "I'm ok," or "No thanks, I'm good."

But now this new gentle boldness was growing inside me. As a patient, I began making new friends at the cancer center. It was awesome watching God work up close and personal to encourage someone else in need. After all, my new friends were experiencing some of the same things as me, so it was natural for us to be able to talk about it. I was excited to share what faith in God could do to help them.

I focused on being a witness for Christ and His healing power by loving others. I spoke enthusiastically of Jesus' love to the lab technicians who drew my blood. They had a positive outlook, too! I chatted with other patients in the waiting area in a powerful, but gentle way. And, I was especially sensitive to listen to those sitting beside or across from me in the infusion room. I loved engaging in conversation, encouraging, bonding, and praying with my new friends. They also encouraged me. The connection was mutual.

Hair Loss
By the fourth round of chemo, my hair started to fall out in clumps every day for two weeks. It was heartbreaking, especially since I was growing my hair long for nearly two years. Suddenly, it was slipping through my fingertips. My beautiful brown curly locks—gone! The hair just knotted up and broke off. I regularly found stray pieces laying on my shoulder or on Jeff's shirt after a loving hug.

The hair loss was more evident when I washed and conditioned it—I no longer used a blow dryer. I dreaded seeing the inevitable handful of hair balled up in my hand shortly after massaging the shampoo into my scalp, and I hoped it would soon stop. To avoid clogging the shower drain, I placed the clump of hair on my soap dish until I could throw it away. I avoided washing my hair daily as I used to, and stretched it to every two or three days—but it still kept breaking off and falling out, so I asked Jeff to cut off about 3-4 inches to lighten the load.

At first, I wept over my hair loss, but then I encouraged myself. I determined it was minor in the scope of things! I wanted to focus on getting better and not hair loss. My youngest sister, Eileen, sweetly offered to shave hers off if mine kept coming out. She encouraged me by saying, "It will grow back! You are beautiful with or without hair. It will grow back!" She was right. Thankfully, I had thicker hair to start, so it ended up thinning out, but not all coming out.

I have an incredible friend and hairdresser, Tara, who gifted me a stylish haircut. When I told her how thin my hair was (before seeing her), she didn't miss a beat. She told me that her hair was thin, too, but assured me there are ways of making it appear thicker. When I sat in her salon chair she comforted me, "I specialize in thin hair." Those well-chosen words ministered life to my soul like pearls of great price. My husband ordered an attractive head scarf in case the hair loss continued, but it didn't.

Support
This faith journey was filled with ups and downs, but all along the way devoted family, friends, and extended family of God were continually lifting us up to the Lord in prayer, sending hundreds of greeting cards (nearly 1,000), visiting, preparing meals, and supporting us with their love, faith, gift cards, and financial blessings. Amazingly, every need was met.

Our wonderful Senior Pastor and Associate Pastor showed us grace by allowing my husband, who is the Facilities and Grounds Manager at our church, the flexibility to be home with me as much as possible until I was strong enough and able to be alone. Thankfully, Jeff's position allowed him to do a lot of his daily work by email and phone.

He also worked a few days a week from his campus office to keep things running smoothly. Our life-long friend, Dennis, who works on Jeff's maintenance staff, lovingly filled in the blanks while Jeff took care of me.

Jeff and I never planned on or expected to have chemo treatments (who does?), nor did we ever think it would come to that point. But it is amazing what you can do and what you can go through, when you have to do it and when there is no other way but to go through it.

I like the saying:

If God brings you to it,
He will bring you through it!

I am a living example of that truth.

We were determined to make this walk through cancer a journey of faith, and it was going to take all of the faith we had, plus the faith of other believers to turn this situation around. **I believe it is never the wrong time to believe God for the right thing.** God could have healed me all at once, but He didn't. He chose instead, a day by day steady progression of faith, healing, and restoration. In the process, Jeff and I learned to cherish each moment together, and Almighty God faithfully walked beside us and held our hand every step of the way.

Adversity

By Germaine J. Hoffman

Adversity opens a window to our soul
And displays all of its contents
Adversity shapes our character
And uncovers every fear
Adversity reveals the heart in refining praise
And its flame does not die out
Until its mission is accomplished and its work is completed.

Adversity takes us higher in Christ
And challenges our faith
Adversity promises no answers
And purposes to deepen our commitment to God
Adversity gives way to greatness
And leaves no stone unturned or uncut
As the Holy Spirit purifies, sifts, and harvests
Eternal fruit that remains.

Adversity develops inner strength as faith defies fear
And righteousness conquers doubt
In adversity believers shout, "The counsel of God is greater than man!
And the Spirit of God is stronger than man!"
Adversity causes us to relinquish our reliance on human wisdom
And redirects us to Christ the Savior for our triumph
Jesus stands cheering us on from His glorious Heavenly throne.

Love is embedded in the heart of adversity
Victory is conceived, perceived, and believed
It is no longer "I" but Christ living in me.

Adversity, God chose you as my teacher,
Look how far you have taken me
And now I can genuinely say, "I BELIEVE!"
Amen.

My giant chocolate
chip cookie

On oxygen...

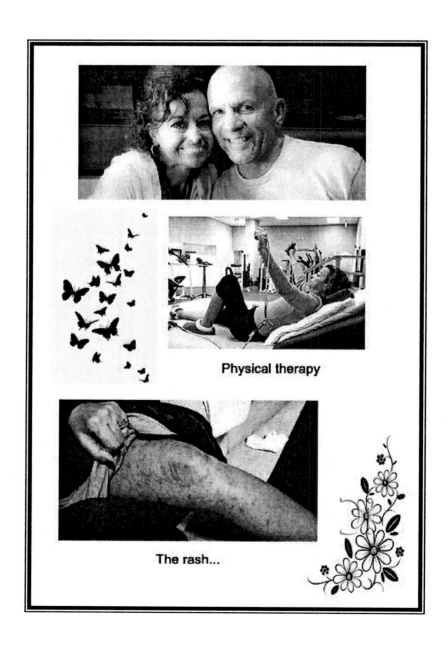

Physical therapy

The rash...

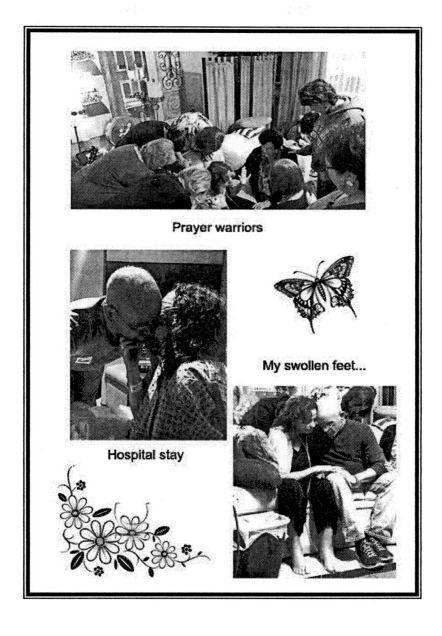

Prayer warriors

My swollen feet...

Hospital stay

Pressing on...

LOVE WINS!

GETTING HEALTHY
AND OFF THE COUCH
Chapter 7

Dreams, Encouragement, and Changes

And it shall come to pass in the last days, says God, that I will pour out of My Spirit on all flesh; your sons and your daughters shall prophecy, your young men shall see visions, your old men shall dream dreams.
Acts 2:17

Dreams

During the constant physical battles, struggles, and challenges that a cancer diagnosis presented, the beauty of the Lord was so evident, and far outweighed all of the ugliness of the disease. **God's grace is greater than cancer.** His victory is stronger. His love is unequaled. His power is made perfect in weakness. He encouraged and assured me of my complete healing through dreams and visions that He gave to me personally and through others.

- My sister Eileen dreamed she was watching a special interest story on TV. A female commentator announced the next segment, "The True Story of Germaine Hoffman." The song "On Christ the Solid Rock I Stand" began playing right after she introduced the story. My sister was left with the impression that this scenario would be played out in my future. I still get God-chills every time I think about it!

- My niece Jessie dreamed she, my nephew Caiden, and her mother (my sister Eileen) came from our home state of Pennsylvania to visit Jeff and me in sunny Florida. All five of us were at the beach and I was running through the sand with a huge smile on my face. She said I looked so beautiful. I was running faster than anyone else in our group. I was completely healed and healthy... I will take that!

- My friend Cassie dreamed I phoned her saying, "I don't have cancer anymore!" (This was significant because I had not seen Cassie in over three years...) To God be the glory!

- My friend Barb called to tell me she was half-asleep in her bed when she heard my voice loud and clear saying, "I'm healed! I'm healed! I'M HEALED!" It was a wonderful moment for her—it was for me, too, just hearing it!

- When I was in the hospital for the multiple blood clots, the pain in my swollen feet made it necessary to stand on one foot at a time. I prayed, "Lord, I want to put both feet on the floor." Shortly after that prayer, the Lord gave me a Heavenly vision. I saw myself running almost flat-footed across the floor. I knew then that I would, indeed, put both feet flat on the floor again and have perfect balance. It wasn't a matter of *if*, but *when*.

Isn't that awesome? These are some of the loving visual examples of God's faithfulness. I thank Him for putting me on the hearts and in the dreams of others. There is a personal God-sized dream for all of our lives:

> *For I know the plans I have for you, says the Lord.*
> *They are plans for good and not for disaster, to give you a future*
> *and a hope. ¹² In those days when you pray, I will listen.*
> *¹³ If you look for Me wholeheartedly, you will find Me.*
> Jeremiah 29:11-13 NLT
> ꙮ
> *The Lord will be found by everyone who is*
> *willing to seek for Him. He is the answer to your prayers*
> *and the complete fulfillment that you seek!*

Whatever you need to help you through your trial of faith, God will be faithful to supply it. He knows EXACTLY what you need and when you need it. GREAT is His faithfulness...

> *Through the Lord's mercies we are not consumed, because His compassions fail not. [23] They are new every morning; great is Your faithfulness. [24] "The Lord is my portion," says my soul, "Therefore I hope in Him!"*
> Lamentations 3:22-24
> ✽

We can never outgive God. We can never outlove Him. We can never outthink Him. We can, however, always trust in His goodness and rely on His love. He is the Great Shepherd who laid down His life for His sheep. He is the Great Physician and The Blessed Hope. God will always do His part without question—we must do ours. BELIEVE.

Even in the midst of adversity God silences our doubts, fears, and unbelief with His presence, peace, and provision. We may find it hard to recognize God's presence at times, and it may even feel like you are in a desert all alone, but that is where faith kicks in. He promised that He would never leave nor forsake us. It is important not to mistake God's silence for abandonment. He is always up to something good, and for our benefit.

Yes, adversity is a spiritual tool that God uses to shape us!

If you are in need of encouragement; fix your eyes upon the Cross. **Let Christ and His love for you become your focus.** Jesus suffered and died so that we might live. His great sacrifice looked hopeless as He was beat, mocked, and scourged. He was nailed to an old rugged Cross as the angry crowd shouted:

> *... "Crucify Him!" [14] Then Pilate said to them, "Why, what evil has He done?" But they cried out all the more, "Crucify Him!" [15] So Pilate, wanting to gratify the crowd, released Barabbas to them; and he delivered Jesus, after he had scourged Him, to be crucified.*
> Mark 15:13b-15
> ✽

While only days before the Gospel of Matthew records:

Then the multitudes who went before and those who followed cried out, saying: "Hosanna to the Son of David! 'Blessed is He who comes in the name of the Lord!' Hosanna in the highest!"
Matthew 21:9
⅋

These Scriptures teach us that we cannot follow the crowds, we must follow God. Man's plan was to destroy Jesus because of jealousy:

For he (Pilate) knew that the chief priests had handed Him (Jesus) over because of envy.
Mark 15:10
⅋

God's plan was to raise Him up in honor on the third day, so He would reign victorious over death and the grave. **God's plan prevailed...**

Encouragement
God gave me another wonderful, encouraging, and tangible expression of His mighty love. He led my friend Lisa to gather a group of women from our church, who are all near and dear to my heart, to pray for my healing. Because I was too sick to meet them elsewhere, they lovingly surrounded me and interceded for me as I sat on my couch in my living room the night before my first chemo treatment. I think the *Living Room* was an appropriate place for prayer since I planned on living and being around for a very long time—God willing!

These women were in complete agreement with me and God's Word. One by one, they prayed prayers of faith and healing over me. I received every word they prayed because their prayers were fueled by the power and love of the Holy Spirit—nothing less than a miracle would do in this critical time; and they came fully loaded with a spirit of faith and grace which permeated every fiber of my being. I also prayed for them and thanked God in advance for my complete healing. Thank you ladies and thank you Jesus! That was an amazing night!

Circle of 24
In addition to this loving prayer group (among many countless thousands of others who were praying for us), there was also a special

prayer group formed by our church's women's ministries called, Circle of 24. The Circle of 24 (25 if you include me) was inspired by a vision the Lord gave to Jeff.

In the vision, Jeff was in our church sanctuary. The worship service concluded and our women's pastor was in the lobby looking for Jeff. From inside the now dark sanctuary, he heard her say, "I'm going to get Jeff!" She began calling out his name while Jeff was trying to remain unnoticed. Suddenly, she bumped into him in the dark, grabbed his arm and said, "You're coming with me, brother!" and escorted him out to the lobby. They were met there by a group of 24 women standing in a circle waiting to pray for him.

After Jeff shared his vision with Pastor Connie, she felt compelled to make it happen, and she did! Jeff is very humble and would not initiate a prayer group like this, but God knew what he needed and, once again, was faithful to supply it. Those are the surprise blessings that mean so much!

Jeff's new role as caregiver involved a lot of time and energy. He was on call 24-7 to help me, and I could not be more thankful. But I realized he needed to have some down time, alone time, friend time, or do-nothing-at-all time. I encouraged him to relax, have fun, and get a release from all of the daily commitments.

So every couple of weeks, he went out to dinner or to see a movie with a friend. (He always made sure someone was sitting with me—we called them our "angels.") Usually, he did not leave me for more than two hours, and, of course, was sure to check on me in between. Because he was so conscientious and committed to me, he chose to forego the one pastime he loves the most—fishing. He felt uncomfortable getting into a boat with his friend John to fish 6-7 hours because he would be unable to get back to me in a reasonable amount of time, in case of an emergency. He always jokes about getting his *Certificate of Completion* (when he gets to Heaven) for being fully devoted to loving me and taking care of me our entire married life. I believe he will have it and more!

Jeff did and does all things well, and this Circle of 24 banded together as one in the Spirit on his behalf. They were faithful and specific in their prayers for Jeff. They were fully aware of the magnitude of his many responsibilities including:

- Advocate with the doctors
- Caregiver
- Chef
- Contact for family and friends
- Coordinator of "angel" schedule
- Example of Christ
- Facebook and group text updater
- Gatekeeper and the "Door" to seeing me
- Giver of my medications
- Grocery shopper
- Keeper of our personal and medical schedules
- Praise reporter
- Prayer requester
- Prayer warrior
- Protector
- Researcher
- Retriever of family and friends from the airport
- Shoulder to lean on and cry on, hand to hold, and ear to listen
- Taker of my vitals (blood pressure, temperature, oxygen and pulse levels)
- Husband, friend, and so much more—all the while maintaining his position as Facilities and Grounds Manager at our church.

WOW! Reflecting on Jeff's varied roles made me wonder, *"Is he super human?"* No, but he was given supernatural strength and grace by Almighty God. It was no easy task taking care of me. He was my left hand and my right. I could never have walked through cancer without his loving care. He is a *doer* of the Word and not a *hearer* only. He was constantly looking for proactive ways to help me.

For example, when I began physical therapy, the therapists used an ice boot to reduce the swelling in my legs and feet and a flexible exercise ring to help strengthen the inner and outer muscles of my legs. Before the physical therapy session ended, Jeff busily searched the internet from his phone, and ordered the ice boot and the exercise ring (which showed up on our doorstep the next day).

When he noticed my balance was off at times and my oxygen level dropped, a sturdy shower bench and strong hand grip faithfully appeared in my bathroom shower to help me stay safe. He bought them in faith and always believed they would be used temporarily and donated later to someone in need.

He also gave me the best gift of all, the gift of his love, faithfulness, time, and great P-a-t-i-e-n-c-e beyond compare. A nurse once said to us, "That's why we call you 'patients'— because you need lots of patience." She was kidding, but it's true...

Changes—Outward Appearance vs. Inner Strength:
Although my physical body was weak, I praised God my spirit remained strong. As I continued the practice of praising God for allowing me to suffer for His Name's sake, I felt myself getting stronger and stronger inside. This inner strength and peace contrasted the stark reality that my family and friends witnessed from the outward appearance. My now frail and weakening body and physical suffering were painting the wrong picture of me. That is not who I was, or who I intended to be. The Lord gave me this incredible analogy that depicts exactly what I was experiencing:

> Looking at my outward appearance was the same as looking into a funhouse mirror. You see a reflection of the person, and that reflection is distorted—the image is either stretched out and wavy, appears ten feet tall, or four foot wide, BUT it is still an image. The real person is standing there as whole as they were before they ever looked into that mirror.

That's how I felt... whole on the inside and believing God for the outside to change—although the outside looked as though it was not going to cooperate.

For the Lord does not see as man sees; for man looks at the outward
appearance, but the Lord looks at the heart.
1 Samuel 16:7b 🕊

Thank God, my body was not in charge—God was!

Remain Faithful

It is important to remind yourself when you are walking through trials and struggles, especially during cancer, turn to God and not away from Him. He wants to love, comfort, and restore you. He has your best interests at heart. If God be for you, who can be against you? (Romans 8:31). God is for you! Even in the midst of the storm, when you are struggling physically, financially, mentally, emotionally, or spiritually, **He is faithful and He will bring your trial to complete triumph!**

> *Fear not, for I am with you; be not dismayed, for I am your God.*
> *I will strengthen you, yes, I will help you, I will uphold you*
> *with My righteous right hand.*
> Isaiah 41:10
> 🕊

Hallelujah! Use God's Word to encourage yourself.

> *But thank God! He has made us His captives and continues to lead us along in Christ's triumphal procession. Now He uses us to spread the knowledge of Christ everywhere, like a sweet perfume.*
> 2 Corinthians 2:14 NLT
> 🕊

You may wonder, *"If I am suffering, how is that leading to triumph?"* God knows what you can bear and He will not take you beyond the point of grace. His grace is sufficient. His power is made perfect in weakness; in our weakness, He is our strength.

Walking with God helps us to overcome obstacles and triumph over tragedies.

There are times that we can work against ourselves in our thoughts and attitudes. For instance, there are people who become angry with God indefinitely—I am talking decades.

Anger is a natural emotion and it plays a valid role in the grieving process when walking through cancer or other life challenges, but unresolved and prolonged anger will try to overtake us and break us when God's plan is to make us better than we are. God can handle our anger, if we choose to give it to Him.

If we choose to linger in that angry place, however, we hurt ourselves and all of those around us who must bear with our angry attitude. If we are hurting, it is up to us to be honest with God. Tell Him, "This is where I am hurting." Allow Him to cleanse you from the anger and heal you from the hurt. Confess any grudge or accusation that we hold against Him as sin. Ask forgiveness. Most of all, *allow Him* to love you back to life.

Your Heavenly Father loves you more than your anger will ever dare to tell you. It is easy to become angry and blame God for our plight. We wrongfully tell ourselves, "IF" God loved and cared about me then surely He would not allow me or my loved ones to suffer through cancer. **But *the truth is*: He both loves and cares for us AND allows some of us to suffer through cancer.**

Remember, He did not spare His own Son, but gave Him up for us all. That appeared to be a cruel act. What loving father allows his son to be crucified? But the thoughts of God are higher than man, and the wisdom of God is wiser than man. The giving up of His only begotten sinless Son is what led us back to a right relationship with Him.

As we learn to cast our cares upon God, He sets us free from worries, anxieties, doubts, fears, resentments, concerns, hostilities, grudges, or even our own unwillingness to *admit* we need help.

Casting all of our cares to God lightens our mental and spiritual loads. He is more than willing to take the heavy part of the burden. Are we willing to surrender it to Him? Holding onto negativity makes life harder, not easier. And trust me, this is not the time to complicate things.

Cancer causes many reactions—physical, mental, spiritual, financial, emotional, and relational. We are going through a lot. Prayer helps us build and strengthen our relationship with God. Speak to Him often. He always provides comfort, healing, help, guidance, strength, forgiveness, protection and restoration. As we reach out to Him for healing, He will give us a new heart of love and faith in exchange for our bitter heart of anger and resentment.

In all honesty, we can become frustrated because we do not understand what is happening to us, around us, or in us, and WHY it's happening to ME?

When we pray in faith believing **we have** what we asked for, the healing power of God moves in to touch and revitalize our entire being. Once we have received this healing touch from God, no one and nothing can take it away—not even cancer.

> *Now this is the confidence that we have in Him,*
> *that if we ask anything according to His will, He hears us.*
> *15 And if we know that He hears us, whatever we ask, we know that we*
> *have the petitions that we have asked of Him.*
> 1 John 5:14-15

God is Our Healer and Restorer
Restoration is a loving and powerful gift from God. It produces much joy and the grace to move on. It gives life back to the one who is broken.

How?

Do you recall the Old Testament book of Job? Job was blameless before God and the richest man in the land of Uz. He had a wife, children, farmhands, animals, and great wealth, but he lost it all except his wife and his life (see Job chapters 1-3).

> *Then the Lord asked Satan, "Have you noticed my servant Job?*
> *He is the finest man in all the earth. He is blameless—a man of*
> *complete integrity. He fears God and stays away from evil.*
> *And he has maintained his integrity, even though you urged me to*
> *harm him without cause." 4 Satan replied to the Lord, "Skin for skin!*
> *A man will give up everything he has to save his life. 5 But reach out*
> *and take away his health, and he will surely curse you to your face!"*
> *6 "All right, do with him as you please," the Lord said to Satan. "But*

*spare his life." ⁷ So Satan left the Lord's presence, and he struck Job
with terrible boils from head to foot. ⁸ Job scraped his skin with a
piece of broken pottery as he sat among the ashes. ⁹ His wife said to
him, "Are you still trying to maintain your integrity?
Curse God and die." ¹⁰ But Job replied, "You talk like a foolish
woman. Should we accept only good things from the hand of God
and never anything bad?"
So in all this, Job said nothing wrong.*
Job 2:3-10 NLT
꒰

The bottom line—Bad things happen to good people.

**Job was tested not because he did something wrong, but he was
tested because he did everything right.** God provided the sustaining
and overcoming grace for Job to go through his trial—triumphantly! In
the end, God gave Job a double blessing:

*And the Lord restored Job's losses when he prayed for his friends.
Indeed the Lord gave Job twice as much as he had before.*
Job 42:10
꒰

Remember, God did not strike Job with sickness. He allowed Satan to
come against him, but parameters were set for the test. Satan was NOT
allowed to take Job's life. We need to walk close to God through the
trial of our faith. He is our protective Shield. Maintaining our focus
includes maintaining our integrity and a thankful heart. The Lord will
not test us beyond our ability to endure by His grace or His ability to
deliver. Several people asked me, "Aren't you mad at God?" "No," I
told them, "I am not mad at God. Why should I be mad at the Healer?
He didn't do this to me. He allowed it, but He didn't do it." I used my
faith in God to maintain my integrity as Job did.

Getting off the Couch
My number one goal during this time of infirmity was getting off the
couch. My energy and oxygen levels dropped so low that I needed to
be on full oxygen for three months. (My oxygen tank went everywhere
I went.) Unfortunately, the constant flow of oxygen caused me to
develop daily nose bleeds which could last several minutes to several

hours. The intensity of the bleeds varied and appeared at random. My friends commonly noticed the nose bleeds before I did. It was slightly embarrassing to be handed a tissue, but I was thankful for their honesty and help. Thankfully, the bleeds eventually stopped.

Fatigue was also a normal part of my new daily routine. Venturing from my couch to the powder room on my first floor (only 25 feet to my right) was a major feat. The view to my left (a head turn away) offered a beautiful view of palm trees, blue skies, landscaped shrubbery, and a reprieve from the routine. Caught between two worlds—my new reality of fatigue on the couch, which I was determined to overcome, and my faith-filled desire to walk out onto my lanai, pain free, to enjoy some fresh air remained a challenge. So for now, I chose to follow God's instruction in Psalm 46:10a, "Be still, and know that I am God..."

Fashion Change
Despite these physical challenges and overcoming any negative thoughts with the healing power of God's Word, I also needed to tweak my wardrobe. Working in and managing a retail store for many years carries with it a desire to be fashion forward. My artful and tasteful clothing I once loved to wear now hung neatly in my walk-in closet untouched for many months. Sweatpants and T-shirts—easy-to-grab and a few dress sizes smaller, but not my style, were my new daily garb and I now kept them stacked on my dresser for easy access. That bothered me a bit, since I always kept everything put away in its place. I chose a new outlook: *"It's all clean and folded, so what does it matter? Don't major on the minors!"*

Normal household routines no longer exist when you have cancer. We need to adjust to our *new normal.* **Flexibility is the key**. If you are set in your ways and resist change (as many of us do), cancer will help you rethink that position. Remember, "He who is flexible shall not break!"

My stylish and trendy sandals and shoes were relinquished for what looked like my father's bedroom slippers. My husband initially gifted me a fun, bright blue pair of furry slippers. Since they reminded me of a cuddly stuffed animal, I considered hot gluing googly eyes on them for fun—but my energy level was too low to attempt it. My sister Eileen also gave me a comfortable tan pair to add to my new collection. I was happy to wear any slipper because they helped comfort my sore and swollen feet, and I was very thankful to have feet. I recalled the saying, "I cried because I had no shoes until I met a man who had no feet."

My accessories changed from bracelets, necklaces, and pretty scarves to an oxygen hose, my wedding band, and a handy supply of tissues. Priorities had shifted. Getting well was what was important, not my fashion desires.

Going to Church
Throughout this walk through cancer, I wanted to be in the house of God, in the presence of God, with the people of God. We were always received graciously, but some people were unsure of what to say when Jeff and I rolled in with my oxygen tank in hand and the tethered plastic hose up my nose and around my cheeks. I knew I needed all of God's grace and strength to make it through this trial of my faith, and to help others understand—*it's still me, everyone. It's Germaine!*

There were times when Jeff and I sat in the back of the sanctuary, so I could easily remove myself from the church service in the event that I started coughing. I wanted to be a blessing and not a distraction or interruption to other worshippers.

For some reason, I became hypersensitive to smells. If I walked into church (or anywhere) and someone was wearing perfume, it seemed as though they dumped the whole bottle on themselves, or ten bottles for that matter.

When driving from point A to point B, the outdoor smells I used to love such as: fresh cut grass, flowers, wood, or evergreens became intolerable. As did the smell of cigars, cigarettes, or exhaust fumes wafting into our window from cars three or four car lengths away. Strangely enough, I never had a good sense of smell—I needed to be on top of something in order to smell it, but that was no longer the case. I now acquired an acute sense of smell, and it was 500% stronger than I would like it to be. Please go away good sniffer!

And, eventually, it did.

Housekeeping Items

I would like to suggest a few housekeeping items, if you will, pertaining to cancer patients. Many asked, "How can I help?" during our walk through cancer. Here are a few practical items that can help in a social setting:

There Will Be Weak Times and Recovery Times for the Cancer Patient—Be Prepared for Both:

- **Weak Time**—I experienced weak times when my body hurt badly from the joint pain, effects of medication, and edema. People at church services (excited to see me) unknowingly grabbed my hands so powerfully at the greeting time I thought I would go through the roof! They meant no harm, of course, but if you know someone with cancer, be gentle. Their body and health is compromised. You may want to shake their hand, but it is better if you don't—unless you ask them first. Once "normal" handshakes (or touches) become much more intensified when we have cancer and cancer treatments. *A hand on their shoulder or a light hug would be more welcome.* The key is to be aware of the delicate physical condition in which their body may be. Keep that note in mind if you are holding a cancer patient's hands to pray or to comfort. These words are spoken from personal experience! I love you all. It feels good to share a small point that can make a big difference.

  Our attitude toward cancer patients must continue to be love—especially if they appear physically different, use oxygen, or need other medical aids. A friend loves at all times (Proverbs 17:17).

- **Recovery Time**—Keep in mind the golden rule: Treat people as you would like to be treated. **Cancer patients do get better**. People do improve. They can gain new strength. When I was able to walk up or down stairs by myself, it bothered me when people continued to usher me—even after assuring them I could do it myself. In fact, walking on my own felt like a MAJOR accomplishment. Check with the person you are trying to help to see what they need. Listen to and heed what they are saying (unless you think they are in danger). Ask yourself: *"Do they need help?"*—OR—*"Do I have a need to help them?"* Both are valid—just be sure to work on the same page. Teamwork makes the dream work!

There are no hard and fast solutions for every scenario, but your understanding and patience will open an honest communication. Trust me, cancer patients want their healing as much as others want to see them healed. The social situations we face as cancer patients can feel just as uncomfortable as it does for those who are called to walk alongside of us. But, we can bridge the gap while we are healing. Let's work together and do the practical things that help to make life easier. **Listen and learn from each other.** If the person truly needs assistance walking upstairs, getting out of their car, or into their seat, please help them. BUT, please remember as people get better and feel better, if they would rather do it themselves, let them try.

Physical Trials
The physical part of this trial was the hardest part for me to endure. I have been a Christian for more than 30 years and I believed the Lord would heal me. This belief was not based on the amount of years that I walked with God, but on the faith He gave me to believe that my healing was already established in Heaven before I saw it manifest on Earth. Even when I felt discouraged at times because of all of the daily nonstop physical symptoms, I never allowed the voice of discouragement to change what I believed in my heart—God would heal me and I believe the same for you.

In my weakness, God was my strength. Remember, I was healthy my entire life. This cancer diagnosis, coupled with the need to heal from my hysterectomy, added a whole new dimension of physical suffering in my life which I had never experienced before.

If you read the introduction of this book *(I hope you did—if not, please take a few moments to stop and read it now)*, I shared our struggle with infertility. Now, the hysterectomy finalized all of that grief. The only thing I said to God after Dr. Sandadi told me the full hysterectomy was necessary was, "Well, God, I guess that's what You wanted for me."

I could verbalize nothing else. That was it. I chose to trust God's wisdom in my life, even though I did not understand it.

I am an overcomer and I know God has victory in store for the upright. Even when I was on my couch for months, I told everyone who visited me, "I am not staying on this couch! This is not for me. I gotta get up and outta here! By Jesus' stripes, I am healed!" I knew NOW was the time for me to USE my faith and I did. I also linked arms with God and an army of believers who helped me to overcome by faith in Jesus' Name. God, His army of believers, and I will link arms with you, too!

Like the woman with the issue of blood who pressed her way through the crowd to touch the hem of Jesus' garment and was made whole, so I, too, was determined to make my way through the crowd of negative medical reports and multiple physical ailments that needed to be overcome to reach the Throne of God.

I touched Jesus' garment by faith in prayer and was made every bit whole. I love the Bible story of the woman with the issue of blood— her persistence was rewarded and recorded in Mark's Gospel:

A woman in the crowd had suffered for twelve years with constant bleeding. 26 She had suffered a great deal from many doctors, and over the years she had spent everything she had to pay them, but she had gotten no better. In fact, she had gotten worse. 27 She had heard about Jesus, so she came up behind Him through the crowd and touched His robe. 28 For she thought to herself, "If I can just touch His robe, I will be healed." 29 Immediately the bleeding stopped, and she could feel in her body that she had been healed of her terrible condition.
Mark 5:25-29 NLT
🕊

Hallelujah! I have to praise Him! That is my story! **I could FEEL in my body that I was made whole**. I knew how great I felt before the trial, how weak I felt during the trial, and how great, once again, I felt when it was over. That can be your story, too! Touch the hem of Jesus' garment by faith in His Name and you will be made whole.

God Will Direct Your Path

There is a path marked out for each of us to follow. We all have a unique set of circumstances and needs. What works for one may not work for another. God did not create us in a cookie cutter manner, but He created us in a divine design. He is a creative God. We need to love, support, and pray for one another and trust the outcome to God. It was important for me to stay true to the leadership of the Holy Spirit even when well-meaning people felt there may be a different mode of healing for me.

If you need wisdom, ask our generous God,
and He will give it to you. He will not rebuke you for asking.
⁶ But when you ask Him, be sure that your faith is in God alone.
Do not waver, for a person with divided loyalty is as unsettled as a
wave of the sea that is blown and tossed by the wind.
James 1:5-6 NLT

Even though our stories vary like the stars in the sky, the principles of Scripture, found in God's Word, apply to everyone. We all have to pray and seek the Lord's will for our treatment and follow through on the specific road that He gives us. How do we know that road? It will be marked with His PERFECT PEACE.

GOD'S WORD
MAKES ALL THE DIFFERENCE
Chapter 8

A Few of My Favorite Scriptures

All Scripture is inspired by God and is useful to teach us what is true and to make us realize what is wrong in our lives. It corrects us when we are wrong and teaches us to do what is right. [17] God uses it to prepare and equip His people to do every good work.
2 Timothy 3:16-17NLT

The Bible is the infallible, inspired Word of God. It is a must and a mainstay in our battle against cancer. When everything else around us is changing, God's Word remains the same. The promises recorded for us long ago, still apply today.

On the following pages, I shared a few of my favorite Scriptures with you. These life-changing verses helped to sustain me during my walk through cancer. I encourage you to read them prayerfully and receive the healing that is available to you through them. I am sure you can add many more!

*I waited patiently for the Lord to help me, and He **turned** to me and **heard** my cry. [2] He **lifted** me out of the pit of despair, out of the mud and the mire. He **set** my feet on solid ground and **steadied** me as I*

*walked along. ³ He has **given** me a new song to sing, a hymn of praise*
to our God. Many will see what He has done and be amazed.
They will put their trust in the Lord.
Psalm 40:1-3 NLT
🕊

There is plenty of action going on in those verses of Scripture. First, there is our part as pointed out by King David, the psalmist. I waited **patiently** for the Lord to help me. Patience is calm endurance without complaint. Second, in this posture of patient waiting, we become aware of the Lord's presence and His great response. He turns to us and hears our cry. He lifts us out of the pit of despair, sets our feet on solid ground and steadies us as we walk along. He gives us a NEW song to sing. He becomes our focus and His joy becomes our strength! And third, I believe, is the pivotal life-changing key—MANY will see what HE HAS DONE and put their TRUST in the Lord. Our entire life is made to glorify God.

Beloved, I pray that you may prosper in all things
and be in health, just as your soul prospers.
3 John 1:2
🕊

For I will restore health to you and
heal you of your wounds, says the Lord.
Jeremiah 30:17a
🕊

STOP: Ponder these Scriptures on divine health for a moment. You are greatly loved by God! Watch Him work on your behalf.

My brethren, count it all joy when you fall into various trials,
³ knowing that the testing of your faith produces patience.
⁴But let patience have its perfect work, that you may be perfect
and complete, lacking nothing.
James 1:2-4
🕊

Going through trials is not easy, but it is possible. As I once heard a famous Christian motivational speaker say, "You can do hard!" I agree. God equips us for the battle through the power and presence of the Holy Spirit and the Word of God. It is amazing what we can endure when we link arms with God, trust in Him, and believe Him for the best outcome. His faithfulness always prevails on our behalf. Our attitude of faith and willingness to believe God to supply all of our needs according to His riches in glory, determines our soaring altitude.

It is also vital to maintain our focus when we are being tested and going through a trial. Ask yourself... *"Where's my focus? The world or the Word of God?"* All of us can get sidetracked or distracted at times, but an honest **daily** evaluation will help us get back on the right track.

> *And they overcame him (the accuser of the brethren, Satan),*
> *by the blood of the Lamb and by the word of their testimony,*
> *and they did not love their lives to the death.*
> Revelation 12:11

🕊

> *Your testimony of God's faithfulness and victory*
> *is vital to the Kingdom of God.*
> *Tell your story and tell Jesus' story of hope and healing*
> *as it is written in the Gospels.*
> *It's POWER!*

❖

God is faithful to His Word, to His people, and to His promises!

> *For God so loved the world that He gave His only begotten Son,*
> *that whoever believes in Him should not perish*
> *but have everlasting life.*
> John 3:16

🕊

God walks with us through everyday life and He speaks to us in a variety of ways. The number one way He speaks to His people is through His Word—the Bible.

One afternoon, I decided to visit a few girlfriends who work at a women's clothing and gift shop. Before I went inside the store, I peeked at the window display. My eyes fixated on a block of wood that was positioned in a corner. Its message read, "But the Lord stood with me and strengthened me...2 Timothy 4:17" How cool is that?

The timely message inscribed on that block of wood was exactly what I needed to hear. I felt God close to me, and my heart leapt with joy. God's Words penetrated deep into my heart and ministered life and health to me at the right time.

God is faithful!

*Therefore, since we are surrounded by such a huge crowd of witnesses to the life of faith, let us strip off every weight that slows us down, especially the sin that so easily trips us up. And let us run with endurance the race God has set before us. ² We do this by **keeping our eyes on Jesus**, the champion who initiates and perfects our faith. Because of the joy awaiting Him, He endured the cross, disregarding its shame. Now He is seated in the place of honor beside God's throne. ³ Think of all the hostility He endured from sinful people, then you won't become weary and give up.*
Hebrews 12:1-3 NLT
✨

Fix your eyes on Jesus… in trials and in good times. Fixing our eyes on Jesus strengthens, encourages, and reassures us of God's presence and faithfulness. Fixing means to direct one's attention, eyes, or mind steadily or unwaveringly—to attract and hold a person's attention or gaze.

Have I not commanded you? Be strong and of good courage; do not be afraid, nor be dismayed, for the Lord your God is with you wherever you go.
Joshua 1:9
✨

O Lord my God, I cried out to You, and You healed me.
Psalm 30:2
✨

But those who wait on the Lord shall renew their strength;
they shall mount up with wings like eagles, they shall run and
not be weary, they shall walk and not faint.
Isaiah 40:31

Where there is no counsel, the people fall;
but in the multitude of counselors, there is safety.
Proverbs 11:14

God offers us help through His Word, His Holy Spirit, and spiritual counsel of godly leaders and pastors. He also provides education and help from doctors and medical personnel. You are not alone. As we mentioned before, God's signature in decision-making will be marked by His peace.

Psalm 91 was the core Scripture God gave me during my walk through cancer. I read it over and over and over again. When I was too weak to read it, I had someone read it to me. It is an endless sea of blessings. Take it into your heart and personalize it as you read it.

Since I would like you to have the entire psalm to refer to at a glance, I have kept it on its own page. You can use the rest of this page to record your personal prayer to God.

Dear God,

_____
_____
_____
_____
_____
_____
_____
_____
_____
_____
_____
_____

Let's read it together…

Psalm 91

¹ Those who live in the shelter of the Most High
will find rest in the shadow of the Almighty.
² This I declare about the Lord: He alone is my refuge,
my place of safety; He is my God and I trust Him.
³ For He will rescue you from every trap
and protect you from deadly disease.
⁴ He will cover you with His feathers.
He will shelter you with His wings.
His faithful promises are your armor and protection.
⁵ Do not be afraid of the terrors of the night,
nor the arrow that flies in the day.
⁶ Do not dread the disease that stalks in the darkness,
nor the disaster that strikes at midday.
⁷ Though a thousand fall at your side,
though ten thousand are dying around you,
these evils will not touch you.
⁸ Just open your eyes, and see how the wicked are punished.
⁹ If you make the Lord your refuge,
if you make the Most High your shelter,
¹⁰ no evil will conquer you;
no plague will come near your home.
¹¹ For He will order His angels
to protect you wherever you go.
¹² They will hold you up with their hands
so you won't even hurt your foot on a stone.
¹³ You will trample upon lions and cobras;
you will crush fierce lions and serpents under your feet!
¹⁴ The Lord says, "I will rescue those who love Me.
I will protect those who trust in My name.
¹⁵ When they call on Me, I will answer;
I will be with them in trouble. I will rescue and honor them.
¹⁶ I will reward them with a long life
and give them My salvation."
NLT

...Nor shall any plague come near your dwelling.
Psalm 91:10b NKJV
🕊

After reading the verse above I said, "Lord, BUT LOOK AT MY LUNGS! The plague (referring to the cancer) is in there. It's in my dwelling." He lovingly listened and responded, "No! The place where you dwell with Me, in My presence, there is no sickness or disease there." What an amazing revelation! God is my dwelling place. In His presence is the fullness of joy.

Believers in Christ have a responsibility to use their active spiritual power and authority to overcome adversity.

You will trample upon lions and cobras;
you will crush fierce lions
and serpents under your feet!
Psalm 91:13 NLT
🕊

Behold, I give you the authority to trample on serpents
and scorpions, and over ALL the power of the enemy,
and nothing shall by any means hurt you.
Luke 10:19
🕊

God gave us His power to **tread** on spiritual lions, serpents, scorpions, and cobras, which represent the devices of Satan. As we learn to *recognize* and discern the enemy's voice and his devices which come against us in the form of doubt, distraction, discouragement, and dismal doctor's reports, we can rise up and speak the truth of the Word of God in faith in the Name of Jesus and take authority over them. I cannot emphasize this enough—**USE your faith!**

Decree and declare out loud in faith, "No, Satan, you will not steal my joy, my peace, my health, my family, my integrity, my finances, or my victory. The Lord God rebuke you. The blood of Jesus Christ is against you. I have victory in Jesus and I am keeping it!"

The Lord and all of Heaven will back you up when you decree and declare the promises of God for yourself. Satan is not the opposite of God. He is a fallen angel cast down to hell. After **Jesus** was crucified, He descended into hell and took the keys of hell and death out of Satan's hand and **rose with ALL power in His Hand**. He ascended into Heaven and is seated at the right hand of God interceding for you and me.

> *...Fear not; I am the first and the last: [18] I am He that liveth, and was dead; and, behold, I am alive for evermore, Amen; and have the keys of hell and of death.*
> Revelation 1:17b-18 KJV

> *Who is he who condemns? It is Christ who died, and furthermore is also risen, who is even at the right hand of God, who also makes intercession for us.*
> Romans 8:34

Even in your weakest hour—use your spiritual authority.

The enemy flees not at the volume of your voice, but at the power and authority of the Word of God. Your voice may be shallow right now, like mine was, but speaking and decreeing God's Word in faith brings the right results. The more you read, study, meditate, and act on God's Word the more your faith will grow, mature, and increase. Your relationship with God will grow and deepen, too!

> *For this reason I bow my knees to the Father of our Lord Jesus Christ, [15] from whom the whole family in heaven and earth is named, [16] that He would grant you, according to the riches of His glory, to be strengthened with might through His Spirit in the inner man, [17] that Christ may dwell in your hearts through faith; that you, being rooted and grounded in love, [18] may be able to comprehend with all the saints what is the width and length and depth and height—[19] to know the love of Christ which passes knowledge; that you may be filled with all the fullness of God. [20] **Now to Him who is able to do exceedingly abundantly above all that we ask or think**, according to the power that works in us, [21] to Him be glory in the church by Christ Jesus to all generations, forever and ever. Amen.*
> Ephesians 3:14-21

> *Therefore submit to God. Resist the devil and he will flee from you.*
> James 4:7
> ✣

The key for the believer is submitting to God's authority first. Satan knows believers have been given power and authority over him and his evil forces. Speak the Name of Jesus and he will flee.

When believers rise up in faith and use their spiritual power and authority, we begin to win the victory and see the triumph!

We have been given an active role to play in our healing process.

Don't give up!

God will help you and He will heal you. Even if you have prayed for many years, you will reap the good things you have sown. **Your prayers and tears are not wasted**. God cares for you—look how far you have come by faith. You are an OVERCOMER! Sow life into your situation. Speak faith. Speak hope. Speak health. Speak victory. Expect to be healed!

If your health struggle has spanned decades, there is still hope! I prayed and asked God to heal you, TODAY! We may never meet in person, but I believe God has a great plan for your life and He is healing you—right now!

Believe and receive your healing by faith in Jesus' Name. Here is the Scripture He brought to my mind for you...

> *Behold, I am the Lord, the God of all flesh.*
> *Is there anything too hard for Me?*
> Jeremiah 32:27
> ✣

Speak to the mountain in your life, command it to move, and it will. It's NEVER the wrong time to believe God for the right thing!

You keep track of all my sorrows. You have collected all my tears in
Your bottle. You have recorded each one in Your book.
Psalm 56:8 NLT

Jesus wants to dry your tears and answer your prayers. Will you take a step of faith now? If you want to know God and experience His love personally, why wait until the end of the book? Let's pray!

Lord Jesus, I want to be completely Yours.
I give myself to You today. I give You my tears and my fears
of the unknown. Please forgive my sins. Heal my body.
Come into my heart to be my Lord and Savior.
I am excited to begin this NEW journey with You!
Amen.

If you prayed that prayer sincerely from your heart, you are now a believer and your name is written in the Lamb's Book of Life in Heaven. All past sins are forgiven and you have new life in Christ.

Therefore, if anyone is in Christ, he is a new creation;
old things have passed away; behold, all things have become NEW.
2 Corinthians 5:17

If you are still contemplating giving your heart to God, I will extend another invitation to you later in Chapter 12. Praise the Lord!

If you want healing and it seems distant, keep believing. Decree it in faith until it manifests. **Remember healing comes in many forms** and **a positive attitude helps bring forth healing**. Find something to thank God for every day!

OUR MIRACLES
Chapter 9

We Walk by Faith, Not by Sight

Miracles come in all shapes and sizes. Some of them are seen so often in this world that we do not even consider them miracles anymore— the creation and birthing of a child, the prodigal son or daughter returning home, or the uniting of husband and wife in holy matrimony as man and woman become one flesh. There are many miracles in the Bible performed by Jesus for ordinary people such as you and me. I think of blind Bartimaeus (Mark 10:46-52), who was being warned by the crowd to be quiet when he heard Jesus was coming. He did not remain silent, but his cry grew louder. Because of his persistence, Jesus stopped and called for him. Then the crowd changed their tune, "Be of good cheer. Rise, He is calling you." When Bartimaeus approached Jesus, the Lord asked him (in verse 51), "What do you want Me to do for you?" The blind man asked to receive his sight, and he did! Jesus told Bartimaeus that his faith made him well. After receiving his sight, he immediately followed Jesus on the road.

Allow me to ask you the same life-giving question...
WHAT DO YOU WANT JESUS TO DO FOR YOU?
My answer to this question was specific: to be pain free, cough free, and cancer free! When Jesus is asking us what we want, I believe we need to be specific. It is different from making a "wish list" for Santa Claus of things we may or may not get, depending on whether we are naughty or nice. When we bravely ask God for healing, we need to ask in faith in Jesus' Name, according to God's will. Since we know **His**

will is healing (physical, spiritual, emotional, mental, and relational), we are assured we do have the specific things we ask from Him. We can thank and praise Him in advance for the answer(s).

Let's break this question down to where we live... Think about your personal abilities and what you are able to do for others. You can only do for them what is within your capacity, naturally (unless God supernaturally enables you). For instance, I am a writer, preacher, teacher, encourager, and prayer warrior, but I am not a carpenter, fisherman, or Olympic swimmer. If you ask me to construct a well-built home, catch a shark (like my husband does), or swim in an Olympic meet, I would not be able to do any of that for you. Those specialties are not within my scope of expertise. However, when it comes to Jesus, we are not talking about approaching someone who is incapable of supplying our needs. We are talking about encountering and engaging in a divine conversation with Jesus Christ, the Son of God who has ALL power in His hand.

He has officially stopped the crowd for you today, and now He is calling your name and asking the question:

What do you want ME to do for YOU?

Can you answer Him specifically?

Lord, I want to know and love You with all of my heart. Lord, I want to be healed. Lord, I want to believe. Lord, I am asking You to heal my family and friends. The Lord will answer those prayers of faith in His way and in His timing. Wait on Him and trust His timing. The clock is not against you, but for you.

Let's consider the woman with the issue of blood again. She was out of money and out of time. She was bleeding for 12 years and she gave all the financial means she had to her doctors (see Luke 8:43-48). She did not get better, but instead she got worse. When she heard about Jesus, she came up behind Him and touched the hem of His garment and was made whole.

Once again, Jesus stopped the crowd and asked (verse 45), "Who touched me?" (He was on His way with Jairus, a synagogue leader, whose 12 year old daughter was sick to the point of death. Jairus pleaded with Jesus to come and heal her and Jesus agreed, but He stopped to acknowledge this woman's need first.) Everyone in the crowd denied touching Jesus, but **He knew someone deliberately touched Him** because healing power went out from Him.

Finally, the woman came forward and confessed she touched Him. She was the one who was looked down on by society because of her issue of blood; the one who was looked at as unclean; the one who had a faded reputation that brought her to her knees in desperation to the only One who could make a difference in her life. Yes, she was the one who dared to press through the crowd to touch Jesus. Jesus did not reprimand her for touching Him, but He uplifted and approved of her faith. He encouraged her perseverance (verse 48), "Daughter, be of good cheer; **your faith has made you well**. Go in peace." WOW!

So, we have Jesus asking blind Bartimaeus, "What do you want Me to do for you?" Bartimaeus tells Jesus he wants to see and Jesus heals him. The one who was blind now sees! Then we have the woman with the issue of blood (we do not know how close to death she may have been) who suffered with bleeding for 12 years and agonized for an answer. Then suddenly, Jesus was in the crowd. She was determined to touch Him and be made whole, and she was! Jesus recognized her faith and valued her touch by stopping to ask, **"WHO touched Me?"**

Jesus meets us where we are.

This woman knew JESUS WAS HER SOLUTION! He was more than a man, she recognized that **He was God**. We need to know the same truth for ourselves—THERE IS A CURE FOR CANCER and every other sickness and disease, and HIS NAME IS JESUS.

I am the way, the truth and the life...
John 14:6a

I knew Jesus was my solution, too! I chose to believe God for a miracle, even if He chose to answer differently from my asking. It's never the wrong time to believe God for the right thing! **When man does all he can do to help, there is plenty of room for what God alone can do to heal.** I always say, "Man helped me, my wonderful doctors included, but GOD HEALED me!" HALLELUJAH!

The Lord allows us to pray for miracles in Jesus' Name, BUT ONLY HE performs the miracle. Believers speak life, healing, and recovery by faith, BUT it is GOD'S RESPONSE to our faith intersecting with His perfect will and timing for healing that brings forth the miracle. **Our salvation and our healing were paid in full at the Cross of Calvary.** This divine intersection is based on the sacrificial and sinless death of Jesus on the Cross. He made it so—His Holy Resurrection, three days later, and the empty tomb prove it!

Hallelujah! We serve the Miracle-Working Savior and He does all things well—for our benefit and for His glory!

Everything He does in us and through us is to bring glory to His Name. Encourage yourself by declaring, "Jesus will do it for me!"

There is a miraculous release of HEALING POWER in the Heavenlies when we BELIEVE and TRUST in JESUS' NAME! There are oceans of blessings waiting for those who will believe.

I believe that the sum total of all of the grains of sands on the shores in the oceans around the globe, represent only a minute part of the vast and infinite capabilities of the healing power of God to move on our behalf.

Count the stars in the sky if you can. God's healing power far surpasses their greatness! He created Heaven and Earth far beyond our natural ability to see, even with earthly telescopes. That is why we need to use our spiritual *Lens of Faith* to peer into the throne room of God to behold His glory, wonder, majesty, and power.

*By the word of the Lord the heavens were made,
their starry host by the breath of His mouth.*
Psalm 33:6 NIV

God is for us and not against us. He has shown and proved His love to you and me over and over again.

I am the Lord; that is my name! I will not yield my glory to another or my praise to idols. ⁹ See, the former things have taken place, and new things I declare; before they spring into being I announce them to you.
Isaiah 42:8-9 NIV
🕊

I am blessed beyond measure that the Lord chose to perform the following miracles (and many others, I am sure) in my life:

MIRACLES
Miracle #1—Healed From the Pulmonary Embolism
My first miracle was making it past the pulmonary embolism in the ICU with my life intact. I went home from that hospital stay hopping on one foot and using a walker because it was too painful to put pressure on my left foot, BUT I went home beating the odds.

Thank God for His healing power and His Mighty Hand of Protection!

Miracle #2—The Turnaround Begins
The day after Jeff's 56th birthday (March 8, 2016) he and my niece Julie (who was visiting us from Pennsylvania), began noticing the physical change in my countenance, and so did I. I started looking, feeling, and sounding like my outgoing, happy, and joyful self again.

I wondered, at times, if I would ever know what it felt like to be "ME" again—meaning taking a shower **without an oxygen hose,** walking at a normal pace **without getting out of breath,** or eating lunch with a friend at a local restaurant **without a restricted appetite** (instead of sitting on lawn chairs in our garage, using a makeshift table—we simply turned a home improvement bucket upside down and voilà! *Mainey's Café*). I envisioned the day when I would leave my box of tissues at home and my normal voice would return. But day by day, **God began to take all of those things away and they became part of my history instead of my destiny! ALL GLORY TO GOD!**

Miracle #3—The Edema Fluid Leaving My Body
My third miracle was the edema fluid leaving my body. There were so many things going on at once. I was still healing from the hysterectomy, but I was supposed to be increasing my exercise and activity level in general. It was problematic while I was in pain to do both. I wanted to walk, but the pain needed to go and so did the edema fluid that swelled my legs and feet. The Lord lovingly spoke to me, "All edema and toxins are leaving your body," and they finally did!

Miracle #4—Completely Healed of ALL Joint Pain
For nearly six months, I had major joint pain. Getting in and out of my bed (I was in pain even before my feet hit the floor), car, and walking to my second floor were daily challenges. My husband stayed by my side or walked behind me to make sure I made it safely to wherever I needed to be.

On April 12, 2016, I was sitting on the couch and **all of a sudden**, I felt ALL of the pain leave my legs. I shook my head and thought, *"What was that?"* I wanted to test it, so I proceeded to walk up the stairs for the first time in months, pain free! I sat down at the top of the steps with tears of joy streaming down my face. My husband came to check on me. I looked up into his blue eyes and asked, "Do you know how good it feels to be pain free?!!" **I have been pain free ever since!** Praise God!

Miracle #5—The Cough Finally Stopped!
After my fourth round of chemo, I noticed that I was coughing much less. With continued medical treatment, persistent fervent prayers, and faith in God's healing power, the relentless COUGH FINALLY STOPPED! Hallelujah!

Miracle #6—The End of Physical Therapy
I began physical therapy in February 2016. My husband felt strongly about it for my physical health, recovery, and well-being. It motivated me to be in an environment which promoted movement, rather than forging through the process at home. The time was well spent. It was physical and social because my therapists, Maurine and Dawn, were so caring. Jeff went with me three days a week for an hour each day. I did a variety of activity—balancing exercises, either in front of a large

floor to ceiling mirror or on a mat; riding a stationary bike; leg presses, to strengthen and tone my muscles; and simple arm workouts using stretchy bands. The inside of my upper arms needed major work due to the rapid weight loss. They became super stringy-looking because the muscle and fat had gone out of them. It felt good to get them back in shape! On therapy days after chemo, I found it harder to rally, so they adjusted my activity level to give me an easier session.

When Dawn realized I was getting stronger physically and breathing normally again she said, "Germaine, you are improving so much, you don't need us anymore." I am so thankful for Maurine and Dawn. They were patient with me even when I had no energy, and all I wanted to do were the exercises which required me to lie on my back and rest while I worked.

Miracle #7—Cancer FREE!
On September 12, 2016, my oncologist told Jeff and me that I was CANCER FREE! At the same time, I said *"goodbye"* to the blood thinner injections (and eventually, I fully tapered off of the maintenance chemo treatments). Hallelujah! I held onto the Scripture in Mark 5:34a NIV which says, "Daughter, your FAITH has healed you." My blood levels and vitals are normal. I am asymptomatic. And, best of all, I feel like myself again! All praise to God, The Great Physician.

Dr. Harwin said, "This rarely happens!" and "You are a completely different person, medically-speaking, than you were when you first came." Yes, I AM!!! Special thanks to him and our entire medical team's wonderful care.

The miracle did happen, and I am so thankful. Together we defied those miserable odds of less than 1% chance of survival with prayer, treatment, and faith in God. I pray for everyone else to defy them as well.

Now faith is the substance of things hoped for,
the evidence of things not seen.
Hebrews 11:1 KJV

The beauty of this miracle is the Lord reassured me by saying, "This will be just a memory. You will have your story, but the rest will be just a memory." (Meaning the physical part would be behind me.) After He spoke those words to me, I saw a truck, and posted on the side panel were the words, "Just a memory." Later that evening, I was watching a TV commercial and noticed at the top right hand corner of the screen the same words, "Just a memory." The next day, I heard the Holy Spirit say in my heart, "Just a memory." I laughed out loud (for real) and said, "I know, Lord. I know! It's going to be just a memory!"

And… it is… HALLELUJAH!

More Good News:
- My oxygen, pulse, blood pressure, and temperature are normal.
- I can lie flat on my back and no longer use a wedge to sleep.
- I can lie on my side and turn any way I want **cough free!**
- I look forward to getting out of bed and walking **pain free!**
- My body is miraculously recovering and I am **cancer free!**
- My weight has stabilized and my appetite has returned.
- My hair is back to normal.
- My blood levels are normal.
- I am not anemic anymore.
- My voice is back to normal.
- I am involved in active ministry and speak at healing services.
- I volunteer weekly at the cancer center and encourage many.
- I can drive my car.
- We returned the oxygen tanks.
- We donated the shower bench to a thrift store.
- We gave the ice boot to someone in need.

God is using all of this suffering for His glory to show others they can be healed, too!

I am testifying everywhere I go to God's great healing power!

I plan to start a Bible conference ministry (in God's timing) to teach the whole Word of God and encourage its practical life application. I will also be emphasizing God's powerful Word of healing. I believe God for great things, far greater than I can ask or think.

This Bible conference ministry has been my dream for many years. I desire to teach and proclaim God's Word in the power and anointing of the Holy Spirit, so the hearers may be drawn closer to God's heart, develop an intimate relationship with Him, and experience His mighty love and grace.

Jesus has brought me closer to His heart, and made the crooked paths in my life, straight, through suffering... He taught me His ways in the furnace of affliction. He paved the way for new ministry and new opportunities that would not have happened if I was not tested first.

I believe, we cannot leave God out of the equation and have the perfect solution. That truth applies not only to cancer, but to all aspects of life.

The God factor matters.

Many are the afflictions of the righteous,
but the Lord delivers him out of them all.
Psalm 34:19

CROSSING THE FINISH LINE
Chapter 10

The Prayer of Faith
Will Save the Sick

So how did we go through all of that? First and foremost, the peace of God which passes ALL understanding was guarding our hearts and minds in Christ Jesus (Philippians 4:7). It was unexplainable, inexhaustible PERFECT PEACE. By God's grace, I chose to walk and live in God's gift of perfect peace when I could have been fretting for my life. Jeff and I never asked *why* this vicious disease entered our lives (although there is no sin in doing so and many of our friends and family members did ask this question).

One of our pastors told me, "You may not be asking, 'WHY?' but everyone around you who knows and loves you is." Jesus, the spotless, sinless, Lamb of God cried out with a loud voice to His Heavenly Father while He hung on the Cross:

> *...My God, My God, WHY have You forsaken me?*
> Matthew 27:46b
> ✒

Selah! *(Pause and think about that.)* I cannot even begin to fathom the pain and agony Jesus faced and endured for us, the *Righteous* for the *unrighteous*, but I am thankful for the grace He provides to His children who face suffering.

You may wonder if I feared death, or asked, "Lord, am I going to die?" Honestly, I never did. Heaven is a reward, not a punishment. The only question I asked was, "Lord, why should I have my reward (Heaven) when there are so many people that need to know You?" That made no sense to me. But again, I chose not to dwell on it. I asked once and let it go. I can fully relate to what the apostle Paul wrote in Philippians 1:21, "For to me, to live is Christ, and to die is gain." God's grace and strength carried me through. He will do the same for you.

Because of the daily grace and peace of God pouring into my soul, I made no time to think negatively, nor did I want to. And like Jeff explained earlier, if any discouraging thoughts came to mind, we gave them to God, and moved on. Yes, we can hear, see, and feel things which can bring us down, but we still have to choose life and live it to the fullest.

*Today I have given you the choice between life and death, between blessings and curses. Now I call on heaven and earth to witness the choice you make. Oh, that you would **choose life,** so that you and your descendants might live!*
Deuteronomy 30:19 NLT

According to God's Word above, we can be delivered from our family's negative health reports. Yes, some diseases and sicknesses are hereditary, but God's power breaks the yokes and the chains of generations. You can call on Him to end the negative health cycles within you and your family circle.

For example, not long after my healing from stage 4 lung cancer for nonsmoking women and a fantastic cancer free report, my husband developed pains in his upper chest. He had a flush feeling from his chest up into his head. His father, Bob (now with the Lord), had heart issues and a quadruple bypass surgery when he was 64 years old. What do you think the first message was that popped into Jeff's brain? I will tell you, *"Something is not right. I hope it's not heart issues."*

He went to a convenient care facility and was immediately sent to the hospital emergency room for further testing. Jeff contacted me to let me know what was going on. When I arrived at the hospital emergency, he was in a backroom area, but I could see him smiling at me through a half-open long, green curtain. After answering a few insurance questions in the waiting area, I went back to the holding room to see him.

The emergency doctor came in and told us, "Due to family history, Jeff, we want to admit you for more testing." We were both surprised, but felt it was better to be safe than sorry. Jeff was given a couple more EKG's which showed a few minor blips. From there, the doctor ordered a nuclear stress test for the next morning.

The Lord spoke to me that night and said, "This testing is for Jeff. It is for his peace of mind. He is going to be fine." I understood what the Lord meant because the seed of Jeff's father's heart issue nestled in the back of his mind. Whenever he had any type of pain in his chest or side, his first thought was, *"I hope there's nothing wrong with my heart."* A few family members used to call it, "the Hoffman's curse"—AKA a bad ticker.

This hospital visit, I snuggled up next to Jeff in his hospital bed, and we slept till early morning. The doctor came in and explained the process for Jeff's nuclear stress test. He said it would be 2-3 hours start to finish. An hour or so after the test was over, the discharge nurse came in to see us and announced, "Your tests are done. Your heart is PERFECT!" Jeff was relieved and so was I. Yes, this good report was music to our ears! A few minutes earlier, I let Jeff know the Lord showed me this whole situation was for his peace of mind. He agreed and said, "It's nice to know I have a good ticker and I am good for another 50,000 miles!" Amen, brother! **The curse stops here!**

Jesus came to break the curse of sin and sickness.

> *For this purpose the Son of God was manifested,*
> *that He might destroy the works of the devil.*
> 1 John 3:8b
> ❦

Amen. Amen. Amen.

We are under the new covenant and the blood of Jesus has provided for our salvation and healing. For any of you who may are fearing, fretting, or thinking you will develop any type of sickness—whether heart disease, cancer, or diabetes simply because it has been in your family line, be encouraged! God wants to deliver you from that fear.

For God has not given us a spirit of fear,
but of power and of love and of a sound mind.
2 Timothy 1:7

Ask yourself... *"Why do I sometimes receive the negative report of sickness more easily than I receive God's higher report of healing?"* What do you have to lose by trusting God and believing for healing for you and your family? Imagine how good it will feel to be relieved of the pain, sickness, symptoms, and suffering and start receiving healing, wholeness, peace and victory over sickness and disease. Exchange the negative medical reports for God's good plan of healing for your life.

God's good plan includes learning His ways and handing down a **new healthy, faith-filled mindset to future generations through a life of faith.** This faith in God has power to transform us, show us new possibilities, and shape our destiny. Our faith becomes active as we choose to put it into practice in our everyday lives and prayer:

When I call to remembrance the genuine faith that is in you,
which dwelt first in your grandmother Lois and your mother Eunice,
and I am persuaded is in you also.
2 Timothy 1:5

Even as we no longer need to carry the negative cycle of family sickness through future generations; it is also important to note that all sickness or physical challenge does not come upon us because we have sinned. Of course, if you abuse your body with alcohol, drugs, or overeating there are natural consequences to those choices. But to assume all sickness or physical challenge comes upon us as punishment for the result of sin is untrue. The Lord reminded me of the account of the blind man in the Gospel of John.

Now as Jesus passed by, He saw a man who was blind from birth.
² And His disciples asked Him, saying, "Rabbi, who sinned, this man
or his parents, that he was born blind?" ³ Jesus answered, "Neither
this man nor his parents sinned, but that the works of God
should be revealed in him."
John 9:1-3

We can never make blanket assumptions about others. Honor God. Pray and believe for healing and trust God to answer better than we can ask. I recommend you read the entire chapter of John 9 to get a personal knowledge of how Jesus works wonders in our lives even when we least expect it.

Try God's plan.
Whose report will you believe?
We will believe the report of the Lord. His report says we are healed.

I would rather live with a positive hope, expectancy, and faith-filled attitude than with negativity, fear, and dread of the unknown.

I love the way Corrie Ten Boom expressed this truth:

> *"Never be afraid to trust an unknown future to a known God."*
> *Amen!*

We take our healing by faith in Jesus' Name. Can I get a witness?

Why Do We Suffer?
That is a BIG question and there are many reasons for suffering—we will consider a few of them. First, **we live in a fallen world** where no one is exempt from suffering. If we lived in a perfect world, this would not be the case. Second, through suffering, **we realize our great need of God** and learn to overcome by faith and perseverance. Third, there is a refining work done in our hearts as **we turn from our ways and yield to the Lord's ways.** God uses and allows suffering for a season to draw us closer to Himself.

The Lord will perfect that which concerns me…
Psalm 138:8a

❧

But, of course, these are not the only reasons we suffer.

Suffering is part of being a Christian. Godly sufferings are unlike worldly sufferings caused by our own wrong choices, or put on us by the wrong choices of others. **Godly suffering brings glory to God through us.** In our trials, God is with us to help us. He cares for us and loves us. He works all things together for our good and the benefit of others—even the rough places! He is our Deliverer. During our darkest trials, we need to trust God to be our Light and Salvation.

He (God) who did not spare His own Son, but delivered Him up for us all, how shall He not with Him also freely give us all things?
Romans 8:32

❧

Suffering touches us all.

*These things I have spoken to you, that in Me,
(Jesus) you may have peace. In the world you will have tribulation;
but be of good cheer, I have overcome the world.*
John 16:33

❧

For those of you reading this, or know someone who may be asking, "Why does God allow suffering in my life?" I received fresh insight from Pastor John Baschieri, my district presbyter. During a message about worship, Pastor John talked about John 4:4, stating Jesus had to go through Samaria. Jesus didn't geographically need to take this route, but He went that way intentionally so he could meet up with the woman at the well. Pastor John explained, **"Jesus takes us a different way than we might have taken, so we can minister to others."**

That is why I believe I went through all that I did.

When someone asks me, "Do you know what it is like to have stage 4 lung cancer?" I can say, "Yes, I do!" And if they ask, "Do you know what it is like to lose your hair, dehydrate, have low grade fevers, be filled with joint pain, have breathing issues, and rely on an oxygen tank to keep going?" I can say, "Yes, I do!" God knows who we will meet and who our circle of influence will be, and He equips us for the journey.

A few Sundays before I heard Pastor John's message on worship, I was standing in the sanctuary during a praise and worship song. I became so lost in the presence of God, for a moment, I forgot where I was. I felt completely alone in the presence of the King of Glory. All of a sudden, beyond forgetting where I was, **I forgot I ever had cancer** and the Lord was showing me and putting into my heart, "That's how it's going to be. You will have your story, but all of the physical part will just be a memory." WOW! I will take that!

Practical Steps Toward Healing:
Since I am a Bible teacher/preacher, I couldn't resist putting together a list of practical and applicable actions the Lord put into my heart as I walked through cancer. Each step will help you to overcome the evil of cancer with the good health of God's Word. We need to do what is needful naturally, like taking our medications, resting, eating correctly, and keeping active, while doing what is necessary spiritually, like praying, praising, and taking in the Word of God to help feed our inner man.

All of these steps were key to seeing my physical healing take place when I had no evidence whatsoever it would manifest. I pray these simple, yet needful, steps help you to receive your healing in whatever area you need it most in Jesus' Name. Amen!

1. **Prayer**—Every day I asked the Lord to give me the strength, grace, and faith I needed for that day—moment by moment and hour by hour.

2. **Praise**—I praised God every day and thanked Him for allowing me to go through this trial so I could help others. Praise keeps us focused on Jesus and not ourselves. In the beginning of this unforeseen journey with stage 4 lung cancer, the Lord told me, **"Don't sympathize with the symptoms."** That helped me greatly.

Sometimes we talk about our aches and pains so much we let them own us, instead of us taking authority over them.

I am reminded of the encounter of the man that Jesus found at the pool of Bethesda in John 5:5-6, "Now a certain man was there who had an infirmity thirty-eight years. ⁶ When Jesus saw him lying there, and knew that he already had been in that condition a long time, He said to him, 'Do you want to be made well?' " That is a good question to ponder…

3. **Word of God**—The Word of God is life, spiritual food, healing, and POWER! Romans 10:17 tells us how to receive faith, "So then faith comes by hearing, and hearing by the word of God." If you want to increase your faith, get into the Word of God, pray the Word of God out loud so you can hear it, and ask the Holy Spirit to help you to put it into practice in your everyday life.

   Whenever an ungodly thought (not in agreement with God's Word) comes to your mind, reject it and replace it with a Scripture. Go on a search and replace mission in your thought life. I use this exercise with the women I mentor. In a few days, their whole outlook begins to shift. Instead of mentally rehearsing a bunch of negative lies, they replace the lies with the truth of God's Word. John 8:32, "And you shall **know the truth**, and **the truth shall make you free.**" God's Word is truth! Believing God's Word and acting on it brings freedom. Jesus said in John 14:6, "I am the way, the truth, and the life. No one comes to the Father except through Me." Opinions, traditions, and thought patterns contrary to God's Word will not cut it. Make a commitment to speak God's Word over your life and your friends and family. Praying God's Word and speaking blessings of His truth increases our faith.

4. **Receive**—Receive your healing, the love of God, and the love of others. No one can receive your healing. You must believe it, and receive it for yourself. Others can pray and believe for you and God will honor their prayers on your behalf, but ultimately you need to come to a one-on-one place with God. Isn't that what you need? Isn't that what your hungry heart is longing for? Your fulfillment and purpose is found in Jesus Christ our Lord. Even if

you have a tough exterior, God knows you have a tender interior. He made you and formed you for His glory. He has placed extravagant value on you through the Cross of His Son Jesus. He heals others, *but* HE IS YOUR HEALER! Reach out to Him and receive His love and healing.

5. **Use Your Faith**—I spoke God's Word by faith, all of the time, whether I felt like it or not. I said out loud every day, "By Jesus' stripes, I am healed!" When I was on the couch, I told everyone, "I am not going to stay here! I have God's work to do!" I was using my faith and seeing past the circumstances. Walking through cancer was my assignment at that time—not staying in it, but walking through it to gain understanding and compassion of what others go through. All things work together for the good, but we know all things are not good.

6. **Testify**—Tell everyone what God has done for you as you walk through the healing process. Find something to thank Him for. The fact that you are still here is reason enough to celebrate. There is no need to wait until the trial is over to testify and praise God. Tell your story as you go, and praise Him in the midst of the storm. He will lift you up in honor.

7. **Encourage Yourself**—Remind yourself God is in control of your life. You are not alone. God is with you. Every detail of your life is known to God. He is a God of order and peace. He is the Master of solutions. Jesus made us more than conquerors! God is strong enough to take you through. I asked God for an overcoming spirit and He gave it to me. He will do the same for you.

When you doubt or have a low day, look into the mirror and say, "With God's help, I am going to make it! All things are possible to those who believe. I believe! I have victory in Jesus. I am strong in the Lord and of a good courage. I will overcome obstacles with the help of God. God is for me!" (God and you make a dynamic team!)

8. **Recall God's Faithfulness**—God is with us in the midst of the storm. He is our Shelter and Hiding Place. Before I walked through cancer, the Lord gave me two visions:

Vision #1—In the first scene, I saw in the distance, a massive body of water heaped up in what seemed like thousands of feet of water coming directly toward me. The water mass dwarfed any skyscraper on Earth to the size of a shoebox and it was completely contained.

In the second scene, I viewed the mass of water from a different angle. I was now inside a small, but strong, nondescript building—through a small window opening (there was no glass in it), I saw the forward and contained motion of the water headed toward me. Outside, there was a small amount of land, dark green evergreen trees, and plant life surrounding the right perimeter of the building. God had set the boundary. The water could only come so far, and no further. The window opening was symbolic of God's faithfulness—to show me **God was my Shelter.** He allowed me to see the trial (cancer) coming at me through the window opening, but kept me safe and dry inside the building He prepared for me. It was like Noah and the ark, except it was Germaine and the building. I believe the building represented my prayer closet and God's protective care.

Vision #2—In the first scene, I saw a large heap of water rising up on the left. It was like a giant wave in the middle of the ocean, but again, it was contained.

In the second scene, Jeff and I were in a small round life boat that should of tipped over or been consumed by the sheer size and majesty of the wall of water, but it never touched us. In fact, our life boat remained sturdy as if it was sitting on a flat surface and it was completely dry inside. There was no fear. God was on our side. He promised that He would never leave nor forsake us, and He kept that promise.

Isaiah 43:1-3a NLT says, "But now, O Jacob, listen to the Lord who created you. O Israel, the one who formed you says, **'Do not be afraid,** for I have ransomed you. I have called you by name; you are Mine. 2 **When you go through deep waters, I will be with you.** When you go through rivers of difficulty, you will not drown. When you walk through the fire of oppression, you will not be burned up; the flames will not consume you. [3] For I am the Lord, your God, the Holy One of Israel, your Savior…' "

We can trust God to be with us in the midst of the trial.

9. **Stay Relational**—Of course there will be times, if you are the one diagnosed with cancer, when you are not feeling well, and would rather be alone. However, it is important to stay in touch with family, friends, and people of like-faith who can encourage you, agree with you in prayer, take you out for lunch, or bring it to you.

10. **Understand Your Role**—Walking through cancer is not easy, but it is possible. Life is a journey! We never know where it is going to take us. It is full of twists and turns, good times and bad times.

Role of the Caregiver:
If you are a caregiver, your role is vital to the health and well-being of the one you are caring for. You are highly valued and greatly appreciated! Thank you for your loving and devoted service. Being sensitive to the daily needs and wants of the person physically walking through cancer is key to helping them overcome challenges and uncertainties. **Your presence is a blessing.**

Cancer gets tough, but be careful not to let it to toughen you in the wrong way. Putting the needs of the cancer patient above your own is a selfless and humble act and creates an environment of mutual trust, respect, and understanding. You can be firm and sensitive, encouraging and honest. Speak the truth in love.

Caregivers need to follow the steps outlined in these practical steps as much as the cancer patient does. Trust God and ask for help when you need it. Be sure to use wisdom and take care of yourself and your own health. You will need times of refreshing, friendships, and at least brief times away from the one you are caring for. (How often and when is up to you—depending on the severity of the needs.) Search out at least one other person who can help lighten your load.

Role of Family and Friends:
Now is the time, if you need to do so, to make peace with your friend or family member that has cancer. Cancer has a way of nudging us to mend broken relationships, and reunites people who may have long been estranged. There is a finality that cancer brings. It is an interruption so strong, we can't ignore it.

Yes, people do get better and that is what this whole book is about—healing—but many times **healing occurs in the most uncommon ways.** When we learn our friend or family member has cancer out of the clear blue sky, we are shocked! What? My sister, cousin, aunt, uncle, parent, or child has cancer? How can that be? They were fine only a minute ago. How horrifying! Yet, we know that is how suddenly life can change. Be there for your friends and family members. Love and support them. Be sure to create a support system for yourself, too, at work, church, school, or senior center.

Cancer is no respecter of persons. It does not care if you are young or old, rich or poor, weak or strong. It comes to rob us of our peace, joy, and health. It is stubborn and wants its way, to which we say an emphatic, "No!"

Watching those we love suffer through cancer can be more difficult than being the sufferer. This has been my personal experience as I watched one of my spiritual mothers, Shirley Francis, missionary to Africa (who raised funds for water wells), endure stage 4 metastasized lung cancer. I had the honor of being with her every day (at least 6 hours) the last two weeks she was here on earth in hospice care.

It was not easy to see her in pain. Sometimes on my drive home, I prayed in my car, cried, and released my pain to God. Then I asked for the grace to go back the next day and do it again.

The Lord's assignment was for me to be a "hand" to her. In obedience to God, and love for my friend, I gave her my hand to hold, to comb her hair, to brush her teeth, to feed her meals, and to take her to the restroom. The Lord said to me, "Jesus loved His disciples to the end. Love her to the end." And I did!

Role of the Cancer Patient:
As a cancer patient, I know it is vital to keep positive and think the best. You are what you think. What you think is what you believe. What you believe affects the way you live. Never give in to despair. If you fall, get up again. Trust God for the best outcome. Be a light! Encourage yourself and those around you. Let everything that has breath in it, praise the Lord!

God gives grace on both sides of this walk through cancer. There is grace for those physically walking through cancer, and there is grace for those helping cancer patients walk through the process. Every relationship is special and unique. Every person is important. It takes a multitude to take care of one person with cancer. Even if you are single, think of all of the nurses, doctors, pharmacists, physical therapists, technicians, family and friends it takes to take care of you and thank them for it. You are greatly loved! One is a whole number!

11. **Ministry of Tears**—Jesus wept (John 11:35). Cry when you need to. God gave us the ability to release our hurts and struggles through cleansing tears. The Bible tells us He puts them all in a bottle, but I think He has a 500 gallon drum reserved for me!

12. **Focus on and Maintain the Victory!**—You will gain the victory as you believe, receive, and proclaim it by faith. The Lord has already provided VICTORY for each of us when He said on the Cross, "It is finished!"

For our light affliction, which is but for a moment,
is working for us a far more exceeding and eternal weight of glory.
2 Corinthians 4:17
🕊

When negative reports come, use your faith, and maintain your victory. The Lord told me, **"Maintaining your victory will be your triumph."** I am holding on to that and never letting go!

13. **Thank God for the Triumph**—Keep in mind, the goal of the trial is to bring glory to God through you! Believe, receive, obey, and decree God's Word over your life and thank Him in advance. He will show up and do the rest!!! 2 Corinthians 2:14a helps us, "Now thanks be to God who always leads us in triumph in Christ…" You are in partnership with God! You are NEVER alone!

Love, patience, and compassion are always helpful and needful as we walk through cancer. Many loving friends came to "give me flowers" while I was living. The aroma of their presence, love, faithfulness, and prayers scented my entire house and my thanks will never end.

14. **Never Give up Hope!**—The Lord knows what we can bear, and He will come through for you right on time. Thank Him for the healing you have already received. Matthew 7:7-8 says, "Ask, and it will be given to you; seek, and you will find; knock, and it will be opened to you. 8 For everyone who asks receives, and he who seeks finds, and to him who knocks it will be opened." NEVER give up hope! Your next prayer could be your breakthrough. I prayed for my husband's salvation for 17 years—it was worth the wait!

The Power of Prayer—A Holy Weapon

> *…The effective, fervent prayer of a*
> *righteous man avails much.*
> James 5:16b
> ❧

Prayer and faith go together. They are cornerstones to our belief in the Living God.

During this walk through cancer, God orchestrated multi-thousands of devoted believers to pray diligently for my healing from Florida to Pennsylvania, to Romania and Italy. How miraculous is that? Faith-filled intercessors prayed fervently, faithfully, and mightily. It amazed Jeff and me! Thank you Jesus!

At our home church, my name was lifted in prayer and live streamed around the world every time the door was open. The Lord also strategically placed people along the way to encourage Jeff and me.

When I was in the emergency room with multiple blood clots in my legs and lungs, a doctor asked if she could pray for me, and she did.

Our women's ministries pastor, Connie Weisel, was extremely faithful and sensitive in our journey. She came to my hospital room, fell to her knees in prayer, and ministered a beautifully meaningful Scriptural communion to Jeff and me. She prayed for us to have the wisdom necessary in making decisions concerning my health and treatment and God granted it.

The woman who administered my pre-admission EKG was a believer and offered to keep me in her prayers. She assured me, "The doctors are going to go in there and take out whatever is necessary and that will be the end of it." How encouraging! She was unaware that I was scheduled to have a baseball size tumor removed. She spoke out in faith and I received the blessing.

After the pulmonary embolism, I went for my follow-up appointment with my primary care doctor who said to me, "It is ONLY God that you are here! Be strong!" Then he looked directly into my eyes and said, "You are strong! I need to be strong!"

God hears and answers every prayer offered in faith.

My brother David texted me the most beautiful prayer: "Germaine, my prayer is total healing for your lungs. Lord, in the mighty Name of Jesus, You are the Great Physician, there is nothing impossible for Your mighty Hand. And Lord, this is a small problem Your servant Germaine has in Your eyes. So I ask You to anoint Germaine from the top of her head to the soles of her feet and show the non-believer Your greatness. May many souls be won for Your Kingdom through her testimony of healing. I thank You, Lord, in advance, because You said, ask and you SHALL receive. And Lord, I am asking and believing. I praise Your Holy Name, Lord, and I thank You, Jesus. Father, in

Jesus' Holy Name give my brother, Jeff, the strength he needs in these difficult times, and anoint my brother with a double portion of Your love and grace in Jesus' Name. AMEN!!!"

Hallelujah! In the beginning of this trial, I invited my dear friend, Lisa, and my spiritual daughters Teresa, better known as "T-baby," and her sister Mary to my house for a night of worship, prayer, and praise. We played Christian music videos and focused on the songs that proclaimed the power in the Name of Jesus! He breaks the chains that would want to keep us bound in sickness. Yes, Lord, do it for me!

We prayed, praised, believed, anointed, and confessed my healing. I am sure all of Heaven was rejoicing with us! We prayed courageously, "Let Your will be done on earth as it is in Heaven." Calling down God's healing power on earth is part of our spiritual inheritance. His will is healing. There is POWER in the Name of Jesus. At the Name of Jesus, every knee will bow and every tongue will confess He is Lord to the glory of God the Father (Philippians 2:10-11).

I am thankful thousands of people were praying and believing for Jeff and me. We also prayed for them. What a tremendous blessing!

If you are not sure what to pray, start with the perfect prayer Jesus taught us. Then use it as a guide to form your own personalized prayer.

In this manner, therefore, pray:
Our Father in heaven,
Hallowed be Your name.
[10]Your Kingdom come.
Your will be done
On earth as it is in heaven.
[11]Give us this day our daily bread.
[12] And forgive us our debts,
As we forgive our debtors.
[13] And do not lead us into temptation,
But deliver us from the evil one.
For Yours is the kingdom and the
power and the glory forever. Amen.
Matthew 6:9-13
🕊

MY FRIEND, DO YOU HAVE CANCER?
Chapter 11

Pearls of Encouragement for Cancer Patients

Getting the diagnosis, "I'm sorry, you have cancer…" is one thing; learning to live and walk through the reality of it, is quite another. Cancer comes with a wide range of emotions and concerns, and rightly so. It is a serious disease that can have devastating effects. Who invited us into this club anyway? There was no notice. No warning sign posted above our front door… We had no way of knowing this malady would ever creep into our lives—even though statistics show one in three will develop cancer in their lifetime. It's hard to believe that we have become one of the three.

In the following pages, you will find a short list of positive insights that I have learned by walking through cancer—I call them pearls. I hope they are as helpful to you, as they were to me, in overcoming some of the negative thoughts, beliefs, and actions that can occur when cancer comes to steal our joy, peace, and our life. Let's face it—there is NO GOOD CANCER! Yes, there are differing degrees and stages of cancer, and a variety of types (too many—over one hundred!)—some more devastating than others, and some more treatable than others, but **NONE of them are good.**

You are far more than a cancer patient; you are a multi-faceted person with feelings, desires, and questions concerning the future. You are also my friend and I want to help you, as best I can, to face this adversity together. We will touch on some of the many issues cancer patients face. It is up to us, the cancer patient and the person, to find healthy and helpful ways of thinking right, which enables us to believe right, live right, and maintain hope for our future.

Pearl #1—God Loves You!
Say these powerful words to yourself, "God loves me!" Did you do it? Perfect! God does not give us more than we can endure—even when, at times, it seems like He does. God's plan for your life is good! He will support you and make you into a more resilient, better, stronger, and God-reliant individual. This posture of faith and trust allows you to rest in His perfect love and will for your life. He does everything right and never anything wrong. God loves you!

It was important for me to remember how much God loved me when the nurses were inserting the IV needles into my veins in preparation for my chemo treatments, blood draws were happening on a regular basis, my hemoglobin and platelet levels were dropping, the oxygen hose and tank were tethered everywhere I went, and the nonstop, morning-until-night cough lingered for months and months. Believe me, I wanted those procedures and symptoms to STOP! Unfortunately, sometimes things get worse before they get better. But always keep in mind, God's grace is sufficient, His power is made perfect in weakness. He will fight for you, deliver you, and defend you. He will heal you right on time.

He is the God of all flesh. There is **nothing** too hard for Him. He can do all things, but fail. **God loves you with an everlasting love.** He loves you whether you love Him or not. **There is nothing you can do or say to stop God from loving you.** Tell yourself again, "God loves me!"

Pearl #2—Conquering the "C" Word
Now that we have journeyed to this place, it is easier to see the huge role we play in the healing process. We need to filter our thoughts and hurts through God's Word, take the necessary medical treatments to

help us get better, and be thankful for family, friends, doctors and medical teams. In addition, believe God for the best outcome, and fight this fight of faith with patience, perseverance, determination, love, and a positive attitude.

Yet in all these things we are more than conquerors
through Him who loved us.
Romans 8:37
✝

God gives each of us a 24-hour period called TODAY. What we do with that time frame determines the quality of life we have and the legacy we leave behind.

I have friends and family members who *conquered* cancer. Some of them told me, "Twenty years ago, fifteen years ago, or ten years ago, THEY gave me six months to live." Did you hear that? Twenty years ago, fifteen years ago, or ten years ago… but they lived far past the anticipated 180 day threshold and were given 7,300, 5,475, and 3,650 additional days, respectively, and counting! These are living testimonies all of us can celebrate! I was also given a less than 1% chance of survival, but here I am—a year later, 365 days past my grim expiration date and still going strong. **It is possible to CONQUER and OVERCOME cancer by faith in Jesus' Name**.

I get excited to hear the good reports of those who have passed the cancer free one-year mark and are now well into their decades, or on their way to it. I can't wait to say, "Twenty years ago, I was diagnosed with stage 4 lung cancer, BUT GOD healed me!" I chose God's report in lieu of the less than 1% statistic. His report gave me 100% chance of survival. His report is recorded in the book of Isaiah:

But He was wounded for our transgressions, He was bruised for our
iniquities; the chastisement for our peace was upon Him,
and by His stripes we are healed.
Isaiah 53:5

Our healing was complete when Jesus hung on the Cross and said, "It is finished!" (John 19:30).

In order to conquer cancer, I chose faith in God and His Word when there was no physical or medical evidence to support me. But GOD, Heaven's army, and the faithful believers on earth had my back. I referred to Mark 10:27b often, "…With men it is impossible, but not with God; for **with God ALL things are possible.**"

Man and medical research can take us so far, God will take us the rest of the way. As I said earlier, we are all given the same amount of time to live on planet Earth and it is up to us to make the most of TODAY. No one is promised tomorrow. Therefore, we set our sights beyond this world and make our Heavenly home our destination as Abraham did, so we can live each day with peace, love, and purpose.

Yet, the sinister voice of cancer is like a viper ready to strike at any moment. It spews its venomous report and is by no means pleasant. In fact, it can be downright frightening if we fail to guard our hearts against it. Cancer lies and shouts, "You have six months to live," or "There is nothing more we can do for you, it's over," and it expects us to concede our victory, eat its lie, and accept it as our truth. We must resist taking cancer's negative report as our own. Instead, we need to cling to the wondrous report of the Lord that **NEVER** changes. "By Jesus' stripes I am healed!" (Isaiah 53:5).

Yes, we need to stand strong in the face of adversity and believe God to back us up and raise us up to total health and strength. It's never the wrong time to believe God for the right thing! There is POWER in the Name of Jesus.

Before David slew the giant Goliath (see 1 Samuel 17:34-37), he first conquered the lion and the bear who stole the sheep out of his field. We must do the same. David struck back and took back what the Lord gave him—**healthy sheep!** My first lion was infertility threatening to devour me and take me down into the pit of despair for keeps, but God lifted me. I have also tackled and conquered several bears called grief, sorrow, and pain.

Jesus conquered every plot and scheme of the enemy who is seeking to devour your body and your testimony. Satan wants you to give up without a fight—he wants you to live each day in fear and dread. He wants you to sink to your lowest low until you become unrecoverable. But, when you call on the Name of Jesus, He will faithfully lift you out of every valley and give you the grace and the strength you need to move on.

Be sober, be vigilant; because your adversary the devil walks about
like a roaring lion, seeking whom he may devour.
1 Peter 5:8

Sometimes we can get *stuck* mentally and it immobilizes us. That's the enemy's plan! He wants to paralyze you spiritually and mentally, so he can overcome you physically and emotionally. **The only way he can win is if we let him**. That's his plan. He wants us to come into agreement with his lies, believe them, and therefore live far below the abundant life Jesus promised to give us.

The thief does not come except to steal, and to kill, and to destroy.
I (Jesus) have come that they may have life,
and that they may have it more abundantly.
John 10:10

Allow the enemy no advantage by proclaiming, "It's hopeless! The negative reports are right. I am going to die. I am tired of this. I give up!"

Exchange your grief and suffering for healing words of life and praise. **Praise will restore your power, energy, health, and quality of life.**

Try this prayer approach instead: "Lord, I do not understand any of this, but I praise You that my life is in Your hands. Thank You for loving me. Thank You for helping me. Thank You for dying for me and providing for my health and salvation. I trust in You even when there is no proof—medically-speaking—that I will get better. I choose to see myself whole and healed in Jesus' Name. Amen!"

The Lord will renew your youth like the eagles and give you peace and grace for each new day.

Let everything that has breath praise the Lord. Praise the Lord!
Psalm 150:6

Put on the whole armor of God (see Ephesians 6) and give the enemy no opportunity to devour you mentally, physically, emotionally, spiritually, or relationally. Disagree with his lies. Stand up and believe God! **You are VALUABLE!** Your life matters! Your life has purpose! Join the countless multitudes before you who received their healing from God. Your life is a gift! Do not let yourself be devoured, displaced, or devalued by a defeated enemy—Satan and his evil forces. **Stay in the fight of faith.** When you are tired or weary, allow the Lord to carry you.

Do not be overcome by evil, but OVERCOME evil with good.
Romans 12:21

I was told many negative things during my walk through cancer. First, I was given a less than 1% survival rate. We know God gave me 100% survival rate. Whether I am living here on this earth, or eternally in Heaven, I am surviving—more than that, I am thriving. Second, I was told this type of cancer is incurable. Again, thank God I know the Lord. He helped me not to receive that report into my heart, or to make it my own. I focused on God's ability to make the impossible possible. **He can heal anyone at any time.** Third, I was informed the next place you see a pulmonary embolism like I had is on an autopsy report… WHAT?? And last, several medical personnel told me they thought they would NEVER see me again because I was so sick and frail— BUT GOD!

Human beings, as wonderful as we are, do not yet know everything, although the medical breakthroughs have been amazing and we have come a long way! There are still many things we need to learn and discover. Patients, doctors, family, and friends are all a part of God's team. God gave man his masterful mind, but He has reserved some things that logic alone cannot answer. Faith pleases God. God spoke the world into existence. By His spoken Word, He created the Heavens and Earth, every creature, tree, planet, star, ocean, and you and me.

There are things that ONLY Our Creator can do and we must humble ourselves in order to allow Him to do them for us.

Thoughtful people sent me hundreds of wonderful, positive, uplifting greeting cards with their thoughts and prayers while I was walking through cancer. But, among them were also cards expressing the "depression and deep sadness I must be feeling." Honestly, with God as my witness, I was HOPEFUL, not hopeless! Why? My body was weak, but my spirit was STRONG!

Of course, I had moments when I cried or felt disheartened, we all do, but I told the Lord whatever was bothering me, released it to Him, and moved on. **I never stayed in the place of discouragement and did not make room in my heart to fall into a pit of despair.** I was too busy praising God for raising me back up again and seeing myself going forward, even when there was no physical evidence whatsoever to prove it! You can too!

Pearl #3—Stop Going to the Internet for Medical Information
It is always wise to be educated and know what you are facing when dealing with cancer, but it can also be detrimental if all we do is go on the medical websites and rehearse all of the horrific things that can happen to us. We can dwell on and worry about "**What if** that happens to me?" scenarios. To that I ask, "**What if** it doesn't?" Satan, the god of "What if," is behind all of those scare tactics, but we serve the Great Almighty God, and His Name is "I AM" (Exodus 3:14).

Make sure you are taking in positive success stories of those who have beat cancer while praying with love and compassion for families who experienced loss. (Jeff and I pray for every person who has cancer every night.) Go to faith-based websites to increase your faith, encourage your heart, and pour positive truth into your spirit. Spend time **building yourself up**, not tearing yourself down, or causing undo heartache. Cancer is tough enough without adding more negativity into the mix. I chose to stay off the internet medical websites, and opted to read the Scriptures to increase my faith and encourage myself. I recommend that if you plan to search a website, choose one that speaks life and healing, not death. Our will is involved.

Pearl #4—Do You Need Prayer?—Ask for It

If you need prayer, like I did, please ask for it. Never assume someone should know what you need. Sometimes people do know you need specific prayer, but there are other times when we need to speak up for ourselves and say, "I could really use prayer today." Reach out to a pastor, friend, or someone with like-minded faith who can help coordinate that for you. There is power in prayer and there is power in coming together in Jesus' Name. He promised to meet us there!

For where two or three are gathered together in My name,
I am there in the midst of them.
Matthew 18:20
♉

Pearl #5—There Is Always Hope!

If you need hope this verse in Jeremiah is perfect to meditate on and memorize:

"For I know the plans I have for you," declares the Lord,
"plans to prosper you and not to harm you,
plans to give you hope and a future."
Jeremiah 29:11 NIV
♉

Our lifespan on earth may grace 120 years, but eternity is forever! **Our future is eternity.** God wants to give us hope for our eternal future in Him, as well as hope for the here and now.

We need to be in a state of preparedness. Is our heart right with God? Do we know Jesus as our Lord and Savior? Have we submitted ourselves to Him and His will for our lives? Have we laid down our burdens at the foot of the Cross and asked the Lord to take over?

Our surrender will go a long way in our healing. Remember when Jesus was preparing for the Cross, He cried out in the Garden of Gethsemane in Luke 22:42, "Father, if it is Your will, take this cup away from Me; nevertheless not My will, but Yours, be done." When we surrender our will to God's will, we receive a Heavenly reply in the form of abundant grace, faith, and joy to walk through the darkest valleys in perfect peace.

Pearl #6—Let's Not Make Excuses

Where are you in the healing process? Are you angry, accepting, grieving, hopeful, hopeless, bitter, kind, faithful, resentful, or maybe a mixture of all the above? Walking through cancer tends to put a reality on our finality and what really matters in life. Honesty is a key component of walking through the process.

As a cancer patient, I tried to express God's love as best I could to as many as I could by letting my light shine and showing appreciation and encouragement to the nursing staff, lab technicians, and other patients. No one can tell another person how to feel about their diagnosis—they have to come to those conclusions for themselves. But it is important to maintain our focus. Keep the door open for healing instead of calling it "quits!"

We can give ourselves many convincing excuses **why** we cannot receive healing: it's too far gone, no one else believes it's possible, or **what if** it doesn't happen?

Remember, it's never the wrong time to believe God for the right thing.

> *Have I not commanded you?*
> *Be strong and of good courage; do not be afraid, nor be dismayed,*
> *for the Lord your God is with you wherever you go.*
> Joshua 1:9
> ✌

As long as there is TODAY, there is ALWAYS HOPE for our healing. We must keep first things first—getting better and back in the game! **Press on valiant soldier!**

People who see me now find it hard to believe I ever had cancer. (So do I!) They are amazed at the litany of ailments God helped me to overcome. It gives them faith, hope, and encouragement to believe that they, too, can receive a miracle. You never know the impact your faith will have on someone else's healing!

I share my story everywhere I go. I have told my hairdresser, nail technician, and even my smoothie maker how God healed me. And, they are amazed!

Facing cancer takes courage and bravery—it also takes many loving arms and listening ears. We draw from each other's strengths and give to one another what is needed in that moment. God also helps us at all times.

> *Blessed be the God and Father of our Lord Jesus Christ,*
> *the Father of mercies and God of all comfort,*
> *⁴who comforts us in all our tribulation, that we may be able to comfort*
> *those who are in any trouble, with the comfort which*
> *we ourselves are comforted by God.*
> 2 Corinthians 1:3-4
> ❧

As a cancer patient, you have the ability to positively impact others. Consider the story you are telling others about yourself. Is it woe-is-me all the time, or is it positive affirmations—"I am going to make it! I am fearless! I am an overcomer! I am holding onto hope! I will beat the odds! I choose a good attitude! If God is for me, who can be against me? I will trust God and fear no evil. He will bring about the right outcome. I place my life in His capable hands."

If you are feeling ill or are in pain, that is perfectly understandable. No one expects you to be a cheerleader on days like that. Sometimes it is better to sit, or lie quietly, and be still and know that He is God. But overall, ask yourself, "What am I doing to contribute to my healing?" Do you speak life over yourself, or do you tend to bow down to thoughts of death and despair? Do you pray, "Lord, heal me"? But then cancel your words of prayer by telling others, "What does it matter? I am going to die anyway!" Let's not make excuses. We need to choose life as God commands and embrace it! Every day matters. Our words matter. Our prayers matter. Our faith matters.

*But let him ask in faith, with **no doubting**, for he who doubts is like a wave of the sea driven and tossed by the wind. ⁷ For let not that man suppose that he will receive anything from the Lord; ⁸ he is a double-minded man, unstable in all his ways.*
James 1:6-8
🕊

The truth is, we are all leaving this earth one day. We just do not know *when.* We need to live every moment to the best of our abilities through the power of the Holy Spirit.

Since we know we are leaving here one day, would you agree it's important that we get ready for the move by getting our hearts right with God? Doing so will help us to live abundantly here on earth, too.

Never allow yourself to fall into the pit of depression so far you begin to believe you are "better off dead." Ending your life is NOT God's will for you. Do not fall into the temptation of the enemy to take your life! We need you! REACH OUT FOR HELP IN EVERY DIRECTION! Talk to your doctor, minister, counselor, family, friend, or call 911, but take action against these negative, life-threatening thoughts. If God be for you, who can be against you? (Romans 8:31) God is for you! Tell yourself, "God is for me!" We need to be *for* ourselves.

Pearl #7—Stages of Grief

There are stages of grief involved with cancer and its treatment—anger, denial, confusion, dismay, unbelief and their counterparts of peace, acceptance, hope, perseverance, and overcoming faith. Of course, the initial diagnosis is a whammy, but there are also grieving stages of longing for the life we used to have. This grief process in and of itself exposes our loss.

For me, simple things like going out for a cup of coffee with my girlfriends became impossible. Everyone had to come to my house. I longed to walk through our neighborhood without getting out of breath, but never made it further than 30 feet into my garage.

Jeff and I could no longer go on a spontaneous date. It took forever for me to get ready, and I was usually too fatigued to sit in a restaurant.

One time we tried going out to dinner, and I managed to enjoy half a meal, when suddenly it all came back up and landed in a napkin. Oh, it was awful! But thankfully there were only a few others around, and the napkin was huge. Things happen! Life happens. We make adjustments.

I was fortunate the nausea and vomiting did not happen often, but it did happen. Those were not fun times, but God took us through it. When I was at my weakest and frailest state, I looked at myself in the mirror and thought, *"Who is that woman? I hardly recognize her... She is so frail and weak."* But in my heart, I knew I could overcome this adversity with faith in God and the right attitude. Let's face it. Life is different when we are walking through cancer! Find ways to be thankful for each small task you can do, instead of mourning the bigger things you are unable to do at the moment. A THANKFUL HEART is a powerful key to overcome obstacles and grief. I asked God for an overcoming spirit, and He gave it to me. You can too!

Pearl #8—Don't Be Mad at Healthy People
If have you cancer, it can be tempting to allow the root of bitterness to rise up against those who do not have this disease. I spoke with people with cancer who acknowledged their anger at healthy spouses for being able to rest, while they could not. (This anger is part of grieving for the life we used to have.) If this speaks to you, next time you are tempted in this way, stop, and reverse the thought. Pray for your caregiver and yourself. Be thankful they can sleep. Caregivers carry a heavy load. They need their strength and energy to take care of you, themselves, and perhaps, others.

Ask God to search your heart. Is there any root of anger, jealousy, or pride lodged inside? Is there anything that needs to be dealt with and extracted by our *Great Physician*? Cancer presses on those areas where we have been unkind, unforgiving, or unloving. Only God can remove these unhealthy roots through confession, repentance, and forgiveness. You can get better!

> *This is My commandment,*
> *that you love one another as I have loved you.*
> John 15:12

⚘

Pearl #9—Do Not Allow Self-Pity to Consume You
Even though you are walking through this great trial, you can choose not to buy into self-pity. It costs too much! There is always someone else who is worse off than you and me. Count your blessings instead of your problems. You will find your greatest struggles being used for good in your greatest victories. It's easy to declare, "Woe is Me!" but this attitude will do nothing to help you get better. Thank God for where you are on the way to where you are going—it's healing!

Any improvement is a plus, and recognizing it is vital to your mental, physical, and emotional well-being. Surround yourself with positive, faith-filled people and allow yourself one temper tantrum a week, or a day if needed, and move on. It takes more energy and thought power to be negative than positive.

*Finally, brethren, whatever things are **true**, whatever things are **noble**, whatever things are **just**, whatever things are **pure**, whatever things are **lovely**, whatever things are of **good report**, if there is any **virtue** and if there is **anything praiseworthy**—meditate on these things.*
Philippians 4:8
🕊

Verbalize positive words and maintain healthy thinking. Listen to uplifting worship music, laugh with friends, color, paint, or open a window and smell the fresh air. Do something you enjoy!

Pearl #10—You Can Make It!
Because Jesus has paved the way for us, you and I can make it! Philippians 4:13 promises, "I can do all things through Christ who strengthens me." You CAN do this. You can do hard. It seldom feels good, but you can make it. My brother David always told me, can't means "won't." If you tell yourself you CAN do it, you will see yourself going up and over every hurdle. **There are no limitations when we believe—only possibilities.** Have you ever watched the Paralympic Games? It always amazed me how fearlessly our brothers and sisters run the race set before them with prosthetic legs. They are true heroes and role models.

> *Therefore we also, since we are surrounded by so great*
> *a cloud of witnesses, let us lay aside every weight,*
> *and the sin which so easily ensnares us,*
> *and let us run with endurance the race*
> *that is set before us.*
> Hebrews 12:1
> ᶘ

If you are in chronic pain or your thinking is cloudy, that is quite different. I believe God gives a special grace for those who suffer in this way—He wants to speak life to you. I pray a special blessing for your complete healing—mind, body, soul, and spirit. Perhaps someone is reading this book to you. Be encouraged! God is able to make all grace abound toward you. HE LOVES YOU WITH AN EVERLASTING LOVE! YOU are HIS PEARL of great price!

Pearl #11—We Are ALL in This Together
No one walks through cancer alone. We are here to help and care for one another! Cancer brings a common denominator. It affects families, friends, co-workers, neighbors, and communities on various levels. Everyone can learn something about faith, humility, and love through the sacrifice that is needed to help someone walk through cancer. You are not alone even when you "feel" like you are. Our emotions are unreliable, but God and His Word never change. Jesus said, "I will never leave nor forsake you." Tell yourself, *"I am never alone. God is with me."*

> *Jesus Christ is the same yesterday,*
> *today, and forever.*
> Hebrews 13:8
> ᶘ

Pearl #12—Keep Learning and Keep Dreaming
Though we may lose some of our former way of life, we also discover new gains. How? Walking through cancer opens new doors in our hearts which might have previously been closed. We *understand* others with new perspective, *listen* with new interest, and *love* with new loyalty. Commitment and genuine humility are fine-tuned in our hearts like the melodic sound of a violin in an orchestra. Cancer does

NOT make these changes happen, but our response to the experience works all things for the good. We start to look for the BEST quality of life we can possibly live.

During my walk through cancer, my number one lesson learned was the VALUE OF LIFE! Not only my life, but everyone's life. Your life is important and valuable. I was ALWAYS thankful for my health, but I now discovered the pearl of great price in my Savior's treasure box—the VALUE OF LIFE. I will wear it with thanksgiving and praise!

I also learned to LIVE FOR ETERNITY. It is my desire to live in such a genuine way that my ears and arms are open to those who need to experience the love of Jesus. His love was always shown in practical ways (like feeding the 5,000) and spiritual ways (pointing us to repentance and restoration to God). God's agape unconditional love (the highest form of love) expressed through us in service to others pleases God!

Loving and serving God and others leads to a life of fulfillment. Ask God for a new dream to dream while you are walking through cancer. My prayer was, "Lord, use me where I am. Let this walk through cancer become a ministry." And it did!

Pearl #13—I Believe You Can Live "Healed" and Still Have Physical Adversity

Healing comes in many forms. Sometimes the healing God gives us may not be physical, it could be **mental**—giving you peace of mind and heart to endure what is necessary at the time. It could be **emotional**—as He weans you off of your feelings and centers you in His Word. It could be **relational**—broken relationships are suddenly mended and changes of heart happen in those we may have been estranged from for years. It could be **spiritual**—you make your peace with God. The dots are now connecting and the pieces of the puzzle are coming together on your behalf.

Cancer causes us to sober up, take an honest evaluation of where we are in life, examine how we want our future to go, and consider what legacy we are going to leave behind for others.

When I was sick in my body, my spirit stayed completely whole—intact. Nothing lacking. I was healed when Jesus said, "It is finished!" on Calvary and gave up His Spirit to His Father in Heaven, and so were you. That is how we can faithfully declare complete victory even if our bodies are uncooperative. I personally know men and women of GREAT FAITH who spent many years struggling through cancer, sickness, or other diseases.

Trust me.

It was not due to a lack of faith.

They prayed, believed, and received answers to many prayers for others. But God still allowed their malady *as He did with Paul's thorn in the flesh* to bring glory to His Name. Their physical condition did not discount *their faith to believe* for healing. They may have received an inner healing that we know nothing about. **God is SOVEREIGN.** *In some cases, we may have questions without answers until we get to Heaven.* He knows what He's doing, when to do it, and how to do it... Our job is to TRUST and REST in His ability to heal in His own way and time.

Pearl #14—Adversity Develops Character

Adversity is a teacher! What we learn from its varying and sometimes heart-wrenching and mind-boggling lessons makes all the difference in our lives. Let's face it... how many of us willingly sign up for the life class called, "Adversity?" Think about what you have learned from your experience. How can this knowledge be used to help others? Are you willing to let God refine your thoughts, attitudes, and actions in order to come forth as pure gold? *The Lord refines every believer He receives in the fire of affliction, and He develops our character in adversity.* He brings glory to His Name through our willingness to lift Him up when we are down. **He is STRONGER than cancer. He is GREATER than adversity.** He is the One who walks on the water and calls us to join Him. Will you step out of the boat (your comfort zone) by faith and trust God to give you the victory?

...but we also glory in tribulations, knowing that tribulation
produces perseverance; ⁴ and perseverance, character;
and character, hope. ⁵ Now hope does not disappoint,
because the love of God has been poured out in our hearts
by the Holy Spirit who was given to us.
Romans 5:3-5
🕊

I have heard it said, adversity does not only develop character, but it reveals our current character. I believe that. It surely revealed mine.

Does your character need refinement? We all need refinement! Examine yourself. Are you jealous, fearful, unbelieving, skeptical or critical? Have you given up your ways and fully submitted yourself to God so that He can develop the fruit of the Holy Spirit within you?

But the fruit of the Spirit is
love, joy, peace, longsuffering, kindness,
goodness, faithfulness, ²³ gentleness, self-control...
Galatians 5:22-23
🕊

The Lord has been working on producing His spiritual fruit in me for many years. When I gave up my resistance to adversity and God's dealings in my life, it was easier to see His fruit that remains. It is the fruit of the Holy Spirit—not self-effort. Think about it—who does not want LOVE, JOY, and PEACE? I do! I am sure you do as well! That fruit will mature naturally as we abide in the Vine (Jesus) and willingly submit to the whole will of God. Surrender brings victory!

The righteous person faces many troubles,
but the Lord comes to the rescue each time.
Psalm 34:19 NLT
🕊

The Lord knows exactly how much pressure can be applied to our lives to bring forth the desired result: our sanctification and healing, a greater faith, and most of all, a closer walk with God. HE IS THE REWARD for diligently seeking Him. Believe God and watch Him work on your behalf.

Pearl #15—Acceptance—A Powerful Healing Tool

When circumstances do not automatically change, we can encourage ourselves by accepting our current situation, but not making it our future. **Accepting where we are on the way to where we are going brings healing.** We acknowledge our struggle, but press on to healing. God is waiting for us to give the heavy weight of our struggle to Him. The burden is not ours to carry. When the divine exchange takes place, we give our heartaches and concerns over to God and trust Him to work all things together for our good in His time.

This is HOLY GROUND…

Many of you reading this book may have experienced the heartbreak of losing your loved one to cancer. It may have been your husband, wife, sister, brother, child, grandchild, or other family member or friend. I, too, have experienced these great losses. Two of my sister-in-loves (sounds nicer than "in-law"); Merie and Joanne, both had brain cancer. My great niece, Laney, had AML leukemia. She was eight years old for five days, and the Lord took her home on Christmas day in 2013. It was shocking and painful. She was a shining star for Jesus and left a mark of love and joy on this planet tens of thousands of people can follow.

It is devastating and **NEVER** a good time to lose someone we love. **Every loss is a great loss, if it is your loss.** Sometimes we try to qualify or compare what scenario is better than another. The truth is, every loss can be difficult. We never want to see someone in pain or suffering. We want to make "it" better, but when we can't, we need to trust our Heavenly Father to help us cope and heal us from our losses. He can put the broken pieces back together again.

I remember when my father went to Heaven. There came a point where my mother so longed for him that she no longer received words of encouragement from me. During our last conversation, she said, "Oh honey, it's so good to hear your voice!" But when I prayed for her at the end of the conversation, I had the sense something was wrong. She was not as receptive as usual. I could feel her pain…

Later that morning as I was getting ready for the day, I looked up to Heaven and prayed, "Lord, I don't want my mom to die, but I give her to You." Two weeks later she left this earth for her new home in Heaven. Imagine my grief as **I now lost both parents**, six months apart from each other. It was more than painful; it felt unbearable. But God helped me through the grieving process and restored my joy over the course of time.

It is a reality and blessing that there is a future glory! Our time here on earth is in God's hands. We need to treasure and value every moment. Even though our loss is great, we need to remind ourselves the separation is temporary and we will be reunited again one day forever.

Place your hurt, pain, and loved ones in the hands of God. Let Him put a healing balm on your aching heart. Heaven is a place with no tears, regrets, or looking back. It is our destination on this journey we call life. It is the ultimate promise of our salvation and Jesus led the way to Glory. Heaven is our reward!

Now thanks be to God who always leads us in triumph in Christ,
and through us diffuses the fragrance of
His knowledge in every place.
2 Corinthians 2:14
✔

Let's Pray... Dear God, Heal the pain of my brothers and sisters who have lost those they love to cancer or other causes. It's NEVER a good time to lose someone you love—young, old, or middle aged. Strengthen those who are nearing or fearing the end. Manifest Yourself and Your healing power to every person reading and receiving this prayer in the Name of Jesus Christ Our Lord. Amen. ❖

THE NEXT CHAPTER
YOU WRITE IT
Chapter 12

Testifying and Overcoming by Faith in Jesus' Powerful, Holy Name

I am thankful to be ALIVE! I feel like Lazarus who was raised from the dead; the grave clothes of cancer are gone, the funeral procession of negative reports is over, and the Resurrection Power of Jesus Christ has raised me up and given me a NEW chance to live and to tell my story.

Before the Lord took Jeff and me through this walk through cancer, I thanked Him continually for my health. But now, every day and every moment of my life became a pearl of great price to treasure, celebrate, and share with others, so they, too, can know the love of Jesus Christ and receive their healing.

God has restored my body to total health and strength—to Him be ALL the GLORY! He has put a NEW song in my mouth and spirit. He renewed my faith, hope, and joy. He shed His love abroad in my heart, so I can have compassion for those who are suffering. He lifted me high above all circumstances and evil forces that were seeking for my demise. GREAT IS GOD'S FAITHFULNESS...HIS LOVE NEVER FAILS...He fights every battle for us and wins!

Through all of the suffering and pain that cancer brings, I learned the VALUE OF LIFE: to appreciate today because tomorrow is not promised—to value and treasure every opportunity to do good—to love and serve God and others—to be the best wife, sister, aunt, friend, follower of Christ, and child of God that I can be—to help others get to Heaven by introducing them to my Lord and Savior, Jesus Christ.

If you do not know Jesus Christ as Your Lord and Savior, God is extending His invitation to you now through His Word:

We are made right with God by placing our faith in Jesus Christ. And this is true for everyone who believes, no matter who we are.
Romans 3:22NLT
🕊

I invite you to pray a wonderful, life-changing prayer of faith with me:

Prayer of Salvation:

Lord Jesus, I want to know You and serve only You. Thank you for dying for me on Calvary's Cross that I might live. Please forgive me and cleanse me from my sins. I turn from the error of my ways and turn my life completely over to You. Be Lord of my life. Help me to follow You in spirit and in truth. Teach me Your Word and how to apply its truth to my daily life. I choose to live for You. Thank You for receiving me as Your child. I am now saved and a new creation in Christ Jesus. I devote myself to living a NEW life for You! Amen.

Welcome to the family of God!

All of Heaven is rejoicing with you, and so am I...

Hallelujah! We serve a victorious Savior who shares His victory with us. You and I are overcomers by faith in the powerful, Holy Name of Jesus Christ!

❖

I would like to close this chapter of our lives with deep gratitude and appreciation for all the Lord has done for Jeff and me during this walk through cancer. It has been a privilege to share our story with you.

Yes, miracles happen every day. God has a miracle just for YOU!

When Jeff obeyed God, his faith intersected with God's perfect plan—my healing—and my miracle took place—even though I had to walk through the process! I'm so thankful God was with us, for us, and not against us. He put a period on the end of the sentence and set a boundary cancer could not cross. He stilled the waters and calmed the seas. He drew us up close to His heart and kept us under His mighty, victorious arms. He covered us, protected us, secured us, and blessed us in every conceivable way. And He will do the same for you. His faithfulness never ends…

Final Faith-Filled Words Written by My Husband:
We truly all need to live by FAITH, not by what man says. Prayer and FAITH in God are what healed my wife. I am thankful to God for His promise—"Stretch out your hand and I will heal her!" And HE DID!!

Miracles Happen When We Pray!

Lord Jesus, bless everyone reading this book who needs a miracle.
Heal them completely from cancer, sickness, or any disease. Give them
the grace, strength, and faith they need to live each new day.
Open doors for them to testify of Your great love and mercy.
Heal them, Father, with Your great love! Let them, with You,
defy the odds and become a SUCCESS story for Your glory and honor.
We know all things are possible to those who believe—
including healing from CANCER.
Grant it to them now by faith in Jesus' Name.
Amen!

Cancer does not have the final say—God does!

We Win!

TESTIMONIALS FROM FAMILY & FRIENDS
Chapter 13

Eye Witnesses to God's Healing Power

No one walks through cancer alone.
Enjoy the testimonies of those who came alongside me during my
walk through cancer. My thanks to each person (you know who you
are) who gave me a hand to hold, an ear to listen, a smile to cheer, a
hug to encourage, a thought to lift, and a prayer to heal.
Thank you!

I am the Lord, who heals you.
Exodus 15:26b NIV
🕊

Family

Our Lord in Heaven took our beautiful sister who was healthy and
gave her strength through an awful time when cancer struck her down
and wanted to take hold of her. But by His divine grace, her will, and
prayer, God healed her throughout the whole process, and brought her
peace and calm every day. She lived with this cancer and now what a
glorious recovery! She was in pain, she suffered, but I always saw a
beautiful smile on her face. Now she can help others with all of her
knowledge of this cancer! She is an amazing woman! She is our sister,
Germaine. I love you more than words could ever say!
—*Debbie Barskey*

🙂

I am so proud that you are my sister! You are an amazing woman with a faith that is unwavering! God is with you and everyone continues praying for you.—*Bob Capone*

❧

These are excerpts from text messages my brother David sent me when I was walking through cancer: November 21, 2015— I love you, sister!!! This cancer is a small problem for a Giant. We serve the ultimate Giant and His Name is Jesus! He is the Great I Am! He is Jehovah Rapha and the Great Physician. I believe He is going to heal you and your testimony will affect millions of people who are going to turn their lives over to Christ. Your testimony is going to bring God glory, honor, and praise. May 29, 2015—Let no man say there is no God! All they have to do is look at what Jesus has done for you. I am in awe of His healing powers and His mercy and grace. I believe!!!
—*David Capone*

❧

From the moment my sister, Germaine, found out she had an incurable cancer, she believed God for a miracle. We all joined together in one accord believing our Heavenly Father, the Great Physician, would come to her rescue. She quoted a famous saying, "If God brought me to it, He will bring me through it," and He will bring glory to Himself. She knew that God had a purpose and a plan for this unexpected trial in her life. Even through the hardest times, and the worst side effects, she still praised God for the outcome, and the outcome was, SHE WINS! To look back now, it is hard to believe she has ever gone through such a horrific ordeal. God has restored her. He is now using her to minister to others going through cancer treatments. She is sharing her testimony and so are all of her family and friends. She is giving others HOPE! To GOD be the GLORY! Thank you, Lord, for your faithfulness in my sister's life and for answered prayers! God be glorified!—*Eileen David*

❧

I watched my sister walk through cancer with strength and courage. She never complained, but kept her faith in God strong through the whole process. I always reassured her that she had love, support, and God on her side! Although, as her sister, watching her physical symptoms was difficult, I knew in my heart, and never doubted, that she would be healed! It is all about baby steps. Healing came to Germaine on a day-by-day basis, not all at once. I told her there was a mountain at her gate, but she would climb that mountain and it would get smaller every day. It would only be a matter of time when she would look back and the mountain that was in front of her would soon fall behind her, and ultimately it would be completely gone—and it happened! Now on to doing what you were born to do my sister— preach and help others! Love you!—*Kathy Leibman*

꙳

I remember reading one of the most difficult text messages ever sent by my Uncle Jeff. As I read it line by line, I became more emotional and could not justify why this was happening. I realized that somebody I loved and cared about, who was just diagnosed with stage 4 lung cancer, was going to go through some of the most difficult times of her life, and I wanted to be there to support her. I told my husband that I was booking a flight to Florida to see my aunt. I watched as she struggled to walk up her stairs to go to bed. During my visit, if we (my Uncle Jeff, Aunt Germaine, and I) made plans to shop or take a short walk on the beach, it was not long before my aunt was too out of breath to continue. She mostly sat on a chair or nearest bench. She could hardly say a few words without coughing repeatedly. It was so difficult watching her struggle for breath, and she ended up on oxygen.

No longer able to joke around like she did my entire life, we had more quiet times and played board games together, especially her favorite word games. But I knew God had another plan for her, and she was not going to stay this way. I watched her go through a round of chemo. That was one of the hardest things to witness. But, with every round of chemo, we saw improvement in her physical well-being.

Ever since I was a baby, my aunt played a significant role in my life. She and my Uncle Jeff spent almost every day with us as we were growing up. I was blessed to have not just an awesome aunt, but a friend who was there to listen, encourage, and support me. My aunt went from being this fun-loving, outgoing, energetic woman to being frail, tired, and weak. The enthusiastic spirit seemed to be taken away from her, but she continued to believe God for a miracle. My mom gave her an iPad for Christmas. Even through the toughest times, we "FaceTimed" daily. It helped keep our communication going since I am in Pennsylvania. This piece of technology kept us connected in a wonderful way—seeing her face made it feel like I was still in Florida going through the process with her.

It was so inspiring to see her fight the fight of faith and overcome this cancer. *As bad as she was is as good as she is.* She is back to her normal, happy, joyful, enthusiastic, smiling self, and telling everyone of her miraculous recovery. I thank God for that!—*Julie Dangleman*

࿇

I was speechless and heartbroken the day I found out my beautiful aunt, who never smoked a day in her life, was diagnosed with lung cancer. I questioned God, "Why her?" I did not understand why He was allowing this to happen. There are people who smoke multiple packs of cigarettes per day, their entire lives, and are cancer-free. Why did this happen to her? It truly broke my heart. I did not ever want to think about losing her. I have always had such a close bond with her. She always knew how to make things better. She always had me laughing and always gave me her unconditional love. She was and is such a cheerful, loving, and beautiful woman of faith. As months went on, it was heartbreaking to watch her go through the struggles. I will never forget the day I was "FaceTiming" with her, how weak, tired, and expressionless she seemed to be. It was the hardest thing I ever had to see. She was not smiling, could not stop coughing, and appeared so fragile. I broke down and cried, because I knew in my heart this was not the Aunt Germaine I know. Every day my six-year-old son, Caiden, and I prayed for complete healing. We gave it to God and believed He was going to heal her. One time, my aunt told Caiden, "Thank you for praying for me Caidy baby. Your prayers worked!" Out of the mouth of a six-year-old he questioned, "It did?" Aunt Germaine assured him, "Yes, it did!" He said, "I didn't think it did, but since you said that, I will keep praying!" He was so happy and encouraged.

Today my aunt is no longer in pain, no longer coughing, she has more joy and peace than ever before, and most importantly, she is able to show others how faithful God is. God is so good and I am so thankful He healed my beautiful aunt. I praised God through all of this, and He was able to help me quit my horrible habit of smoking. I am one year and three months smoke-free! I love you so much, Aunt Germaine, and am so thankful God brought you through this victoriously!
—*Jessica Behm*

࿇

Spiritual Daughters

❧

I saw my spiritual "mama" go through many trials—physical, medical, and emotional. Through the world's eyes, what she was going through seemed impossible to overcome, but to those who love the Lord, we know with God all things are possible. Through mama's struggle, I saw a faith that moved mountains. The body of Christ united and believed for a miracle. We watched a godly couple stand on God's Word despite the obstacles and negative doctor's reports. They loved one another so completely and always believed the report of the Lord which says, "By Jesus' stripes," mama "is healed." She already had the victory. She is a mighty woman of God who did not "sympathize with the symptoms," as the Lord instructed her. Rather, she believed the Word of the Lord, and showed those of us looking on the true meaning of faith and courage. The woman with the issue of blood in the Bible was not healed solely because she touched the hem of Jesus' garment, but she was healed because *she believed*. Germaine, my "mama," always believed and encouraged us by praying for us when she was at her weakest. To God be the glory! I am forever thankful for our miracle of faith! I love you with all my heart, your "Tbaby."—*Teresa Stabler*

❧

Mrs. Germaine is an exceptional woman of faith. Her walk with God speaks volumes of her character. She has a tremendous love for God's people and prayer. She has given much to many. She is my mentor, and spiritual mother, and I have come to know God in a greater way because of her teachings. I remember when the cough began. We kept trying to figure out what could be causing it—was it allergies, or a cold? We were confused because she was a healthy woman who never smoked. I also remember the day I saw her diagnosis on Facebook. My heart melted, I felt sadness, and overwhelmed with fear. What would happen? Our "chats," as I called them, were about my own healing, but now the one God used to bring healing to my life was sick, and we needed to put our chats *on hold* for a season. I did not know how to approach the situation. I wanted to encourage her, but instead I was encouraged. Her words of faith in spite of all she was facing were amazing. She told me, "The medical report has to come up to my faith level!" She was not moved. The months ahead were not easy; she faced the cough, chemo, and general sickness that comes with lung

cancer. She continued to stay positive and minister to others. God's Word did not fail her—in our weakness, Christ's power is made perfect. Her healing journey is an inspiration to many, including me!
—*Juanita Komoro*

৵

Germaine, "mama," is a gift to us all and an inspiration to many. She is a brilliant and glowing light in this world that can be so dark. She frequently plays the role of thoughtful friend, encourager, mentor, and teacher. Her life is a beautiful example of God's love in action. She has been the hands and feet of Jesus to me countless times and in immeasurable ways. Her life echoes her steadfast love for the Lord. She is a God-pleaser and a God-seeker. She has always been an example in the faith of a woman who knows her God intimately, and she is not only a hearer of His Word, but she is a doer.

When Germaine was first diagnosed with cancer, her response was astounding. Many close to her were shocked, afraid, and even uncertain. Despite being shocked herself, her reaction was filled with hope, perseverance, faith, peace, poise, grace, and God's strength. She encouraged us more than we did her! It was as though she was prepared for this battle—especially spiritually. She believed in God in her confession and her action. Not only in the better seasons of life, but in one of the most difficult times. The most important thing I learned from Germaine's walk through cancer was her response to it. *She was not shaken.* She taught us all that it is not a matter of *if* we go through difficulty, but *how* we go through the challenge that matters. Her response was based on complete faith and trust in the God who she knew loved her... and her response was a lesson for us all. So many times when her situation looked so bleak, she amazed us all with her tenacity to not give up, stay positive, believe God for healing, and ultimately, to walk by faith and not by sight.—*Mary Walsh*

Friends
৵

Watching Germaine and her ever faithful husband, Jeff, go through this time of daunting illness and darkness has been inspiring to those of us looking on, standing with them in prayer. Their story is one of God's strength coming through in times of absolute devastation.

Faced with an overwhelming health crisis, most of us would head for the hills or burrow into the sand, hoping to separate ourselves from the reality of a cancer diagnosis. But when this nightmare came to Germaine's doorstep, she chose to meet the challenge, armed with the Word and holding on desperately to the sword of faith. Although, at times, she may have endured multiple side effects, and been weak in her body, this brave soldier battled through the daily fight with hope in Jesus Christ, her True Physician.—*Pastor John Baschieri*

I can only imagine that it must be a stunning moment when your physician announces you have nonsmoking lung cancer in a serious, and potentially fatal, stage. Such was the case for my friend, Germaine Hoffman. Though a strong believer in Christ, she began to suffer pain, trauma, and onslaught of the terrible disease. She along with her marvelous husband, Jeff, by her side, came to my office to relay the depths of the diagnosis with me. I shared a story of faith with them of how a family member of mine was healed of cancer and prayed with them for her total healing. Germaine determined in her spirit that she would be healed and she "fought the good fight of faith," kept her resolute belief in the healing power of the Master, Jesus, and declared for all to hear that she would overcome and has truly come through victorious. I am thankful and proud for her convictions, her ongoing service to the Lord, and her victory. God has showed Himself strong on her behalf and that is something we can all celebrate together.
—*Pastor Dan Betzer*

I will never forget the day when my friend, Germaine, communicated to me that she had been diagnosed with lung cancer. She told me, "We will beat this by the blood of the Lamb and the word of our testimony." Throughout her ordeal, I never heard her complain. She always kept the faith and believed, and did not "sympathize with her symptoms." She was not moved by negative medical reports. On a daily basis, she declared the praises of the Lord, read the Word of God, and spoke the Word of life over her situation. She never wavered in her faith. She called things that are not as though they were. Without faith it is impossible to please God. She took God at His powerful Word, bringing much glory to Him!—*Carmen Bressler*

My dear friend, Germaine Hoffman, certainly has overcome more trials in the desert than anyone else I know. Through it all, Germaine never stopped reading the Word of God, and standing on its truth and healing promises. She praised the Lord through the greatest trial of her life and her strong faith never wavered even when she did not see God's healing power outwardly manifested. She has come forth as pure gold and is a shining witness for Jesus Christ and all of His faithfulness.—*Julie Faircloth*

❧

When I learned of Germaine's stage 4 lung cancer I was heartbroken. I knew God could heal her, but my faith was weak even though I thought it was strong. Would He heal her? Her faith was STRONG!

She handled this major health trial that tested her faith daily with a courage, peace, and trust in God that I have never seen before. She chose to minister to, pray with, and encourage me and others, when I least expected it due to her illness, which would have devastated most people. But GOD saw her faithfulness, her refusal to accept negative reports, and her love for others in her darkest hours. Because of her brave, positive reaction during her suffering, my faith has grown so much stronger, and my tendency to complain has decreased significantly. I never heard Germaine complain.

The faith, hope, and love this beautiful, humble, faithful servant of God displays is contagious! Many are going to be filled with hope, encouragement, and faith (just like me) once they hear about her walk with God during an extremely difficult time.—*Jill Good*

❧

I saw Germaine on her first day of chemo treatment. She was on oxygen, coughing, could hardly talk, weak, and thin. She remained positive, "Jesus will see me through this. He is my Father, Healer, and Strength. He will heal me." She praised God and quoted Scripture, "By Jesus stripes I am healed!" At her weakest point, she came to our women's Bible study class and encouraged everyone to praise God in the midst of the storm. She declared, "Jesus is healing me! He wants me to help others. He wants me to tell my story!" Gradually, she became stronger, felt better, stopped coughing, and continued praising God! May God bless you, Mainey, and your unfailing faith. Go and help others as Jesus directs you, through your Bible teachings, testimonies, and giving God all the glory!—*Kappy King*

All I can say is how amazing it has been to watch Germaine and Jeff as they have battled the disease that was raging within Germaine. As I stood by her side, I found myself being encouraged and uplifted by their unwavering faith. It was tough; it was painful; it was unbearable at times, but Germaine's spirit stayed strong. She truly became a walking miracle as she shared God's grace, power, and healing touch, even when it was not visible. I praise God for His continued healing of her body and for truly keeping them strong and fearless as they faced this enemy called cancer. Cancer is not and never will be greater than the living Christ that is within her.—*Phyllis Lefort*

🦋

It was nearly 10:00 p.m. when I arrived at Germaine's house from Pennsylvania. There she was, my longtime friend, propping herself up on the sofa to show me how happy she was to see me. I was overjoyed to see her, knelt down in front of her, and we hugged. This hug was the start of my new journey. I knew the Lord was working miracles because my childhood friend talked to me for hours. This was highly unusual for her now because her energy was so low, she coughed so much, and simply asking for a glass of water could send her into a coughing fit. But for some beautiful reason that I can only say was God's gift to me, my best friend, my forever sister, was able to share her heart with me. I listened closely and learned about her steadfast, unwavering love for the Lord. She shared the moment she gave herself to God and the joy it brought to her life.

When Germaine's friends, the prayer warriors, came to pray for her the night before her first chemo treatment, I was amazed. I took photos, with my eyes filled with tears, from all the love I was feeling from each woman's prayer, every one more beautiful than the last. I went to sleep knowing I witnessed something Heavenly.

When I returned several months later, things were different. Germaine and Jeff met me at the airport together! What? She looked like an angel standing there all smiles in the terminal waiting to hug me. This was a life awakening hug for me. I was ready to receive Jesus as my Lord and Savior, but not in the airport, God had plans for later. Being with a minister who is ill with cancer gives you a real lesson in faith and the love of the Lord.

Germaine stood tall and told cancer that GOD would heal her. She did not see it any other way. And because she did not see it any other way, how could I look at it any other way? She is my rock and best friend in the world. She is a minister and the friend I flew all by myself to see because I love her. I do not doubt one word she says. I know she is right because she lives by example. My dear sweet friend continued doing God's work, one day at a time, by praying for and encouraging others, even in the midst of her own trials.

Then it happened! While we were sitting on the sofa talking, Germaine asked me if I knew what "eternal life" meant. I simply said, "No." She explained it to me and said God wanted me to know Him personally. We prayed a prayer of faith and I became a Christian. God is so good!

I am thankful for my Florida sister. I know that I am a work in progress and if my life were not so rich with the Lord, I would never know how poor I would be without Him.—*Tara Rearden*

৯৯

When those of us who love "G" (as I affectionately call her) were shocked that she was diagnosed with stage 4 nonsmokers lung cancer, there was amongst us a lot of crying and disbelief that such an unexplainable cancer was attacking her body. But, from the beginning of this trial, I saw G's unshakeable and great faith in action to move mountains. I have also seen the great faith of her husband, the "Rock," as we call him, lovingly care for and believe with his wife for her healing. "We have a mustard seed and we are not afraid to use it," Jeff would say with a smile and a firm resolve.

The journey has not been easy. I have been by her side in some really rough moments through chemo treatments and at times when she was in excruciating pain. But even in the depths of difficult suffering, because G loves and knows her Heavenly Father so well, she has been steady, strong, and immovable in her faith and trust in Him.

We talked early on that when Jesus prayed, "Thy will be done on earth as it is in Heaven," that in Heaven there is no sickness and we are all healed, so that is His will for us here on earth, too. Our faith has now been become sight. G's heart is to live her life for God's glory, and I have seen her walk through cancer with a grace and strength that can only point to our Heavenly Father. I know that with every breath He's given her with this miracle that the faith of many will be encouraged and strengthened for God's glory.—*Lisa Sadler*

❧

When I first heard my sweet God-sister, Mainey, was diagnosed with—of all things—lung cancer for nonsmoking women, I was in shock. I simply could not wrap my head around those words, it was like someone struck me in the stomach so hard that I could not breathe. I started to cry, went straight to God, and I began asking questions and then even demanded answers (not my first rodeo with cancer). His quiet response deep in my spirit was, "My child, have faith in and watch Me." The words of Deuteronomy 7:9 NLT came to mind, "Understand, therefore, that the Lord your God is indeed God. He is the faithful God who keeps His covenant for a thousand generations and lavishes His unfailing love on those who love Him and obey His commands."

I prayed for Mainey every day, many days I cried for her. It was so hard to watch what she was going through, how this cancer was trying to take my sister away little by little. Each time I received an update, I would go to God and beg Him to heal her. I didn't want a *normal* healing either. I wanted her to be completely healed on THIS SIDE of Heaven. This was my selfish prayer. This incredible woman of God is my sister, my friend, and my mentor. I am not ready to lose her. I would end my prayers with, "Thy Will be done," because ultimately I know it is God's Sovereignty that reigns. This journey has brought me closer to Mainey, Jeff, and most importantly to God. God still answers prayer today!! Mainey is healed in His Name and by His Stripes!! —*MaryJo Soska*

❧

Watching Germaine go through this difficult time showed me that we ALWAYS have hope in God. We all witnessed a true miracle happen with her healing. Jeff and Germaine encouraged us by showing their strong faith, trust in God, and being patient through it all; knowing God provides all we need. The psalmist proclaimed in Psalm 56:3, "Whenever I am afraid, I will trust in You."—*Robin Subbert*

❧

I am astounded at the faith and courage this amazing woman maintained during her entire walk through cancer. From the beginning cough to treatment after treatment, I only heard Germaine speak in faith and stand on the Word of God. When a group of us surrounded her to pray (when she was at her lowest point), she was weak, frail, and on oxygen; she followed up our prayer by praying for all of us! She is amazing, faith-filled, and healed by faith.—*Jeanie Turner*

❧

Germaine and I have been best friends and sisters in the Lord for nearly 30 years. Her love for Jesus and people is genuine. When I visited her in February 2016, watching her suffer, hearing her cough, and seeing her struggle to walk up the steps was painful for me, so I asked God for strength. Her confidence in God's healing power was contagious. SHE lifted my spirit with her amazing faith that did not waver at all. HER courageous hope in God was hope for me. Without a doubt, I knew she trusted the Lord with all of her heart and was not leaning on her own understanding, or the understanding of the doctor's reports. Germaine never took her eyes off of JESUS. She knew where her help and strength came from. She is a beautiful Proverbs 31 woman with an amazing faith in the Lord. Her testimony and faith will bring many out of darkness. Germaine is a beautiful, anointed woman of God with a husband who is anointed and amazing, too! I love them both and know they will continue to let their light shine. To God be the glory for what He has done!
—*Barbara Walton*

❧

I remember well the first day I sat with Germaine as she held in her hands a devastating report regarding the condition of her lungs. Thankfully, nearly 30 years before this trial began, she had come to know and trust Jesus Christ as Savior, Healer, and the God of His Word!

She already knew she could trust Him to take her through to victory. One Thursday morning, after one of her doctor's appointments, Jeff was led by the Holy Spirit to stop by my Bible study class to let the women who had been praying for her see how she was doing. After being seated, she talked to the ladies about her trial and encouraged them to praise God in the midst of the storm. After she spoke and we prayed for her, I told her, "You have been well prepared for this!" That line resonated in her spirit. She knew God was doing a great work and trusting Him for complete healing. She did not know then how fierce the fight of faith would be on this journey, but she was determined to continue trusting God.

After a Saturday night church service, as I sat to pray with Germaine, I told her what the Lord spoke to my heart during service—that He was healing her in a way similar to that of the blind man Jesus healed in John 9:6-11. Jesus spit in the dust, made a paste, applied it to his eyes, and sent him to wash in the Pool of Siloam. The man went (from the Temple Mount...all the way down through the City of David)...he washed...and he was healed. He had to "walk through" from where he was to the place of the completion of his healing. Germaine, with Jeff by her side every step, continued to walk to the "pool of complete healing." All glory to God! Jesus is still the Healer!—*Connie Weisel*

❧

When I first heard of Germaine's diagnosis, I was devastated. And honestly, shocked! How could God allow such a beautiful servant, who wanted nothing more than to serve her God, to be cut down like this? But as the Apostle Paul writes in 1 Corinthians 13:12, I was seeing only in a mirror, dimly. Over the months of struggle, pain, and various treatments, never once did Germaine waiver from her deep faith in a loving and caring God. Even in her darkest days, she offered praise and gratitude for every moment. Even more, she encouraged those of us who were supposed to be encouraging her! From the beginning, she declared the victory in Christ and never moved from that position. Looking back, it makes perfect sense because Germaine has always been a true follower of Jesus, seeking His Word, resting in His promises, and declaring His truths throughout her life. When this trial came, she had been prepared for it from the beginning. I am in awe of her deep devotion to Jesus and her abiding faith. Father God, thank you for this beautiful example of a truly faithful woman. I am honored to call her sister and friend.—*Claire Young*

❧

I have known Germaine for quite a while. She is a strong believer, a gifted encourager, and an anointed teacher of God's Word. I consider her to be a sister, not only in Christ, but in life. I went numb inside when I heard that she was diagnosed with stage 4 lung cancer. I did not know what to think or what to say or even what to do. Those brief few days in the beginning were such agony for me that I could not imagine the thoughts or feelings Germaine and her husband were dealing with. Surely God was not going to let my Sissy die. I don't think I prayed for a day or two because I could not wrap my mind around the fact that He even allowed cancer near her. It was as if God was letting me decide if I was going to believe for her healing or give in to that awful diagnosis. This is something I would have thought only the believer who was fighting for their life had to decide, not their loved ones as well. But isn't it just like God to use these moments to teach us spiritual truths!

Well, who was I not to believe God for Germaine's healing? Of course, I had to believe! Doesn't His Word tell us, "By His stripes we are healed"? Doesn't His Word tell us that every sickness, disease, and infirmity was taken to the Cross with Jesus? YES, it does! And, YES, I believed His Word just as I knew Germaine did even more so. It was as if I had to make a spiritual, conscious decision in my heart to be able to join her in her journey. By doing so, I was blessed to witness firsthand miracle after miracle. Sure, there were setbacks, but the victorious spirit God anointed Germaine with did not allow her to stay down long. *She knew that she knew that she knew God was healing her.* Healing was in the process and it would come to completion so she praised her way through, even during the awful months she dealt with incredible amounts of pain, not being able to breathe without an oxygen machine, and not able to walk for any length of time. For a season, she was only a shell of her former self, but even then she believed God's Word and kept giving Him thanksgiving for healing, and giving Him all the glory for strength and victory. There was only ONE outcome and it was healing!

To look at her now, it is as if she was never sick. God is so faithful! He has already used this journey Germaine had to travel to increase other's faith, draw them closer to God in their relationship, and even believe for their own healing! Germaine and Jeff are the real deal. They are real people who believe in an amazing God and want others to know Him, too.—*Sheri Aws*

I have heard your prayer,
I have seen your tears;
Surely I will heal you.
2 Kings 20:5b

Done with chemo!

In Loving Memory
Chapter 14

Three Champions of Faith

Delaney "Laney" Brown
December 20, 2005-December 25, 2013
Parents: Jennifer and Jeremiah Brown
Siblings: Kylee, Jacob, and Logan

❧

My great niece, Laney, was the kindest, gentlest little lamb, and she left way too early. She loved pink, sparkly things, ballet, animal prints, and alligators. Oh, how I miss her! When I asked her if she was going to be a nurse like her mommy, Jen, she responded, "I want to be an oncology nurse, so when kids' hair falls out, I can tell them, 'Don't be afraid!' " Everyone believed Laney would be healed, and we wanted her here with us, but God chose to take her home where she is ultimately healed and whole. She lived every day happy, joyful, and expecting to get better. She had a fantastic attitude and her life touched everyone from friends, family, nurses, doctors, and her entire community to people around this globe.

Jordan Sadler
August 10, 1995-June 14, 2014
Parents: Lisa and Rick Sadler
Brother: Christian

❧

Jordan was a gentle, kind young man. He lived for God and lost his life with two of his best friends in a tragic car accident soon after his graduation from high school. His love for life and people were evidenced everywhere he went. He was a nephew to me and is greatly missed. His mother, Lisa, had this inscription placed on his earthly resting place, "He was like David, a testimony of God's goodness and grace."

Rebecca "Becky" Soska
October 4, 1981-November 20, 2000
Parents: MaryJo and Bob Soska
Brother: Joe

৵

Becky had a heart for the hurting and those in need. She enjoyed outreaches to feed the poor and homeless. She prayed and talked to those she served. When a poor man stopped and asked her church team, "Why do you care about us and give us free food? We ain't nobody." As Becky hugged him, she responded, "Jesus loves you and so do I." When Becky was diagnosed with leukemia in February 2000, she was determined to overcome her diagnosis. She told her mother, "Mom, if God cures my cancer here on earth, I win. But mommy, if He takes me home to live with Him, I win BIG!" Becky's dream was to open a retreat house for abused kids to teach them about the love of God by using animals. Her greatest desire was for everyone to know Jesus as their Savior. That dream lives on in those who share her story and were touched by her life.

And now abide faith, hope, love,
these three; but the greatest of these is love.
1 Corinthians 13:13

৺

✝

Laney, Jordan, and Becky are champions of faith who made it into Heaven way too soon, but their legacies live on through family and friends. They all loved the Lord dearly, moved mountains with their faith, loved others greatly, and exhibited a strong, courageous humility that speaks volumes without words. They are shining stars and heroes of faith. They pressed on and lived graciously for the glory of God, even in the face of adversity.
Let's follow their example of unconditional love.

A Place To Give...

†

Laney's Legacy of Hope
In honor of Delaney "Laney" Brown
www.Laneyslegacyofhope.org

Laney's Legacy of Hope is a non-profit foundation that raises awareness and funds for pediatric cancer by helping families in financial need and by donating to pediatric cancer research.

†

JJJ Scholarship Fund
www.goecs.org/donate

JJJ stands for Joe, Jordan, and Jonathan: best friends who lost their lives in a tragic car accident shortly after graduating from Evangelical Christian School in Fort Myers, FL. The JJJ fund honors the boys' desire to help upper school students who are being forced to leave the school due to no fault of their own, such as family illness, financial hardship, or family tragedy.

†

Becky's House

Email: maryjo.soska@confidenthopeministries.com

Becky's House is a ministry in the seed stage and it will eventually be established to honor Becky's desire to give families and kids a safe and fun place to go to peacefully retreat from all of the complexities of cancer. Updates to come.

To contact Germaine
for speaking engagements,
please email her at:
Germainesmiracle@gmail.com

*And they went forth, and preached every where,
the Lord working with them, and confirming the word
with signs following.
Amen.*
Mark 16:20 KJV